T0383716

Decolonizing Data

This book focuses on the values and effects that are operational in data technologies as they sustain colonial and imperialist legacies while also highlighting strategies for resistance to autocratic regimes and pathways toward decolonizing efforts.

Systems and schemes for databases and automated data flow processing often contain implicitly Westernized, autocratic or even imperialist features, but can also be appropriated for resistance and revolt. Algorithms are not strictly mathematical but also embody cultural constructs. Values circulate in systems along with labels and quantities. This entails more critically reflective data practices, whether in government, academia, industry or the civic sphere. The volume covers a critique of the data colonialism thesis, which frames computer science as a colonizing science that uses data to classify and govern us, an alternate framing of metadata as "data near data" to challenge seemingly neutral technical terms and a case study of the use of social media platforms in the 2018 Sudanese uprising.

Scholars and students from many backgrounds, as well as policy makers, journalists and the general reading public, will find a multidisciplinary approach to questions posed by data decolonization research from the fields of communication and digital media studies.

Michael Filimowicz is Senior Lecturer in the School of Interactive Arts and Technology (SIAT) at Simon Fraser University. He has a background in computer-mediated communications, audiovisual production, new media art and creative writing. His research develops new multimodal display technologies and forms, exploring novel form factors across different application contexts including gaming, immersive exhibitions and simulations.

Algorithms and Society
Series Editor:
Dr Michael Filimowicz
Senior Lecturer in the School of Interactive Arts and Technology (SIAT) at Simon Fraser University.

As algorithms and data flows increasingly penetrate every aspect of our lives, it is imperative to develop sufficient theoretical lenses and design approaches to humanize our informatic devices and environments. At stake are the human dimensions of society which stand to lose ground to calculative efficiencies and performance, whether at the service of government, capital, criminal networks, or even a general mob concatenated in social media.

Algorithms and Society is a new series which takes a broad view of the information age. Each volume focuses on an important thematic area, from new fields such as software studies and critical code studies to more established areas of inquiry such as philosophy of technology and science and technology studies. This series aims to stay abreast of new areas of controversy and social issues as they emerge with the development of new technologies.

If you wish to submit a book proposal for the series, please contact Dr Michael Filimowicz michael_f@sfu.ca or Emily Briggs emily.briggs@tandf.co.uk

China's Digital Civilization
Algorithms and Society
Edited by Michael Filimowicz

Decolonizing Data
Algorithms and Society
Edited by Michael Filimowicz

Information Disorder
Algorithms and Society
Edited by Michael Filimowicz

For more information on the series, visit: www.routledge.com/Algorithms-and-Society/book-series/ALGRAS

Decolonizing Data

Algorithms and Society

Edited by Michael Filimowicz

Routledge
Taylor & Francis Group

LONDON AND NEW YORK

First published 2023
by Routledge
4 Park Square, Milton Park, Abingdon, Oxon OX14 4RN

and by Routledge
605 Third Avenue, New York, NY 10158

Routledge is an imprint of the Taylor & Francis Group, an informa business

British Library Cataloguing-in-Publication Data
A catalogue record for this book is available from the British Library

Library of Congress Cataloging-in-Publication Data
Names: Filimowicz, Michael, editor.
Title: Decolonizing data: algorithms and society/edited by Michael
    Filimowicz.
Description: Abingdon, Oxon; New York, NY: Routledge, 2023. |
    Series: Algorithms and society | Includes bibliographical references and index.
Identifiers: LCCN 2023009413 (print) | LCCN 2023009414 (ebook) |
    ISBN 9781032290720 (hardback) | ISBN 9781032290737 (paperback) |
    ISBN 9781003299912 (ebook)
Subjects: LCSH: Information technology—Social aspects. | Databases—Social
    aspects. | Metadata—Social aspects. | Imperialism.
Classification: LCC HM851 .D4327 2024 (print) | LCC HM851 (ebook) |
    DDC 303.48/33—dc23/eng/20230313
LC record available at https://lccn.loc.gov/2023009413
LC ebook record available at https://lccn.loc.gov/2023009414

ISBN: 978-1-032-29072-0 (hbk)
ISBN: 978-1-032-29073-7 (pbk)
ISBN: 978-1-003-29991-2 (ebk)

DOI: 10.4324/9781003299912

Typeset in Times New Roman
by Apex CoVantage, LLC

Contents

Contributors

Ulises A. Mejias is Professor at the State University of New York, Oswego. His research interests include critical data studies, philosophy and sociology of technology, and political economy of digital media. He is the author of *Off the Network: Disrupting the Digital World* (2013, University of Minnesota Press) and, with Nick Couldry, of *The Costs of Connection: How Data Is Colonizing Human Life and Appropriating It for Capitalism* (2019, Stanford University Press). From 2021 to 2025, he serves as a Fulbright Specialist.

Kyle Parry is Associate Professor of History of Art and Visual Culture at the University of California, Santa Cruz. He coedited *Ubiquity: Photography's Multitudes* (Leuven University Press, 2021) and is the author of *A Theory of Assembly: From Museums to Memes* (University of Minnesota Press, 2023).

Mustafa Hashim Taha is Associate Professor in the Department of Communication, College of Arts and Sciences, American University of Sharjah, UAE. He taught integrated marketing communication, research methods and conflict and crisis communication. His research interests include framing, media representation of minorities, crisis management and uses of new information and communication technologies (ICT) for social development. Before joining academia, Taha worked as a diplomat in Ethiopia and at the UN headquarters in New York. He also worked in the UN peacekeeping operations in Somalia and Liberia. He wrote numerous articles and book chapters and contributed to many international conferences dealing with communication and media studies.

Series Preface

Algorithms and Society

Michael Filimowicz

This series is less about what algorithms are and more about how they act in the world through "eventful" (Bucher, 2018, p. 48) forms of "automated decision making" (Noble, 2018, loc. 141) in which computational models are "based on choices made by fallible human beings" (O'Neil, 2016, loc. 126).

> Decisions that used to be based on human refection are now made automatically. Software encodes thousands of rules and instructions computed in a fraction of a second.
>
> (Pasquale, 2015, loc. 189)

> If, in the industrial era, the promise of automation was to displace manual labor, in the information age it is to pre-empt agency, spontaneity, and risk: to map out possible futures before they hap-pen so objectionable ones can be foreclosed and desirable ones selected.
>
> (Andrejevic, 2020, p. 8)

> [M]achine learning algorithms that anticipate our future propensities are seriously threatening the chances that we have to make possible alternative political futures.
>
> (Amoore, 2020, p. xi)

Algorithms, definable pragmatically as "a method for solving a problem" (Finn, 2017, loc. 408), "leap from one feld to the next" (O'Neil, 2016, loc. 525). They are "hyperobjects: things with such broad temporal and spatial reach that they exceed the phenomenological horizon of human subjects" (Hong, 2020, p. 30). While in the main, the techno-logical systems taken up as volume topics are design solutions to problems for which there are commercial markets, organized communities, or claims of state interest, their power and ubiquity generate new problems for inquiry. The series will do its part to track this domain fuidity across its volumes and contest, through critique and investigation, their "logic of secrecy" (Pasquale, 2015, loc. 68), and "obfuscation" (loc. 144).

These new social (rather than strictly computational) problems that are generated can, in turn, be taken up by many critical, policy, and speculative discourses. At their most productive, such debates can potentially alter the ethical, legal, and even imaginative parameters of the environments in which the algorithms of our information architectures and infrastructures operate, as algorithmic implementations often reflect a "desire for epistemic purity, of knowledge stripped of uncertainty and human guesswork" (Hong, 2020, p. 20). The series aims to foster a general intervention in the conversation around these often "black boxed" technologies and track their pervasive effects in society.

> Contemporary algorithms are not so much transgressing settled societal norms as establishing new patterns of good and bad, new thresholds of normality and abnormality, against which actions are calibrated.
>
> (Amoore, 2020, p. 5)

Less "hot button" algorithmic topics are also of interest to the series, such as their use in the civil sphere by citizen scientists, activists, and hobbyists, where there is usually not as much discursive attention. Beyond private, state, and civil interests, the increasingly sophisticated technology-based activities of criminals, whether amateur or highly organized, deserve broader attention as now everyone must defend their digital identities. The information systems of companies and states conduct a general form of "ambient surveillance" (Pasquale, 2015, loc. 310), and anyone can be a target of a hacking operation.

Algorithms and Society thus aims to be an interdisciplinary series which is open to researchers from a broad range of academic back-grounds. While each volume has its defined scope, chapter contributions may come from many areas such as sociology, communications, critical legal studies, criminology, digital humanities, economics, computer science, geography, computational media and design, philosophy of technology, and anthropology, along with others. Algorithms are "shaping the conditions of everyday life" (Bucher, 2018, p. 158) and operate "at the intersection of computational space, cultural systems, and human cognition" (Finn, 2017, loc. 160), so the multidisciplinary terrain is vast indeed. Since the series is based on the shorter Routledge Focus format, it can be nimble and responsive to emerging areas of debate in fast-changing technological domains and their sociocultural impacts.

References

Amoore, L. (2020). *Cloud ethics: Algorithms and the attributes of ourselves and others.* Duke University Press.

Andrejevic, M. (2020). *Automated media.* Taylor and Francis.

Bucher, T. (2018). *If. . . Then: Algorithmic power and politics.* Oxford University Press.

Finn, E. (2017). *What algorithms want: Imagination in the age of computing.* MIT Press. Kindle version.

Hong, S. H. (2020). *Technologies of speculation: The limits of knowledge in a data-driven society.* New York University Press.

Noble, S. U. (2018). *Algorithms of oppression.* New York University Press. Kindle version.

O'Neil, C. (2016). *Weapons of math destruction.* Broadway Books. Kindle version.

Pasquale, F. (2015). *The black box society.* Harvard University Press. Kindle version.

Volume Introduction

Michael Filimowicz

Systems and schemes for databases and automated data flow processing often contain implicitly Westernized, autocratic or even imperialist features, but can also be appropriated for resistance and revolt. Algorithms are not strictly mathematical but also embody cultural constructs. Values circulate in systems along with labels and quantities. This entails more critically reflective data practices, whether in government, academia, industry or the civic sphere.

Chapter 1—"Notes on the Historiography of Data Colonialism" by Ulises A. Mejias—presents historiographical inquiry into the data colonialism thesis, emphasizing why the thesis may still be useful for analysis and action despite some of its limitations. Data colonialism frames computer science as a colonizing science that uses data to classify and govern us. Decolonizing and declassifying data from digital networks allows us to examine their social and cultural logics. Colonial and capitalist systems are tenacious and persistent, and their extractivism spans the globe. Data colonialism restricts our imagination by offering us a vision of a homogenized present, suppressing the truth that the past and future are contested fields open to many interpretations.

Chapter 2—"Metadata Is Not Data About Data" by Kyle Parry—argues that the dominant conception of metadata as "data about data" requires rigorous critique. The chapter proposes new approaches to thinking about metadata that are required as a response to the expansion of social media, digital surveillance and persistent calls to dispute and decolonize seemingly neutral terms of discourse. Using ideas from visual culture and Trinh T. Minh-Ha's distinction between "speaking about and speaking nearby," the chapter analyzes metadata beyond the frame of aboutness and introduces the provocation of "data near data." Metadata is not merely data about data but is also distributive, reparative, expressive and extractive.

Chapter 3—"Social Media Use in the Sudanese Uprising, 2018: Mediating Civilian-Military Discourse" by Mustafa Taha—presents an exploratory study examining the influence of social media in the Sudanese revolt that overthrew Gen. Omer Al-Bashir on April 11, 2019. The pro-Islamic Bashir regime censored local media and political dissent, which failed to quell popular unrest. Participants in the protests used social media to coordinate their activities and overthrow Bashir's dictatorial administration. The demonstrators bypassed the blackout using mobile phones, SMS, brochures and word-of-mouth. The study contributes to cyber-activism research on social media in postcolonial contexts.

Acknowledgment

The chapter summaries here are in places drawn from the authors' chapter abstracts, the full versions of which can be found in Routledge's online reference for the volume.

1 Notes on the Historiography of Data Colonialism

Ulises A. Mejias

Introduction

This chapter is based on a lecture delivered at the Histories of Artificial Intelligence symposium, Cambridge University, July 15, 2021.[1] As such, its main concern is with the methods and practices of doing history in the field of artificial intelligence (AI) and computer science, particularly from the perspective of a theoretical framework called "data colonialism" developed by Nick Couldry and myself (Couldry & Mejias, 2018, 2019, 2021). Some of the questions I am interested in addressing are: *What should be the method, or historiography, for doing histories of computing and AI? Can data colonialism serve as a model for this historiography? What do we gain, and what do we lose, by using this method to frame computing as part of a colonial science?*

In essence, this chapter attempts a critique of the concept of data colonialism itself. It has been four years since the publication of our thesis, and in that time we have encountered many productive responses which have allowed us to develop a more nuanced argument and present a more complete history of the "decolonial turn" in data and technology studies (Couldry & Mejias, 2021). At this juncture, I would like to attempt what R. G. Collingwood, in his *Essay on Philosophical Method* (1933/2005), describes as an *internal* critique. An internal critic attempts to "work from within" the argument, in an attempt to "bring to completeness . . . a theory which its author has left incomplete" (pp. 219–220).

Data Colonialism: An Overview

Couldry and I define data colonialism as *an emerging order for the appropriation of human life so that data can be continuously extracted from it for profit* (Couldry & Mejias, 2019, p. xiii). We are not against all data, nor are we saying that data is bad; we are specifically concerned about the commodification of data extracted from our social lives. To put it simply, whereas once the global race was to grab land (and the material resources that went with it), today it is a new resource—data—that is being grabbed and, through it, direct access to the flow of our daily lives and experiences.

DOI: 10.4324/9781003299912-1

But why is colonialism necessary to frame this problem? Why can't we just refer to what is happening today with data as a new form of capitalism?

The data colonialism thesis takes the roots and precedents for what's happening today with data very seriously. The argument is certainly not grounded on a *metaphorical* use of the word "colonialism" to suggest some sort of large-scale injustice. Far from saying that what is happening with data is *like* colonialism, or *resembles* colonialism at a superficial level, the data colonialism thesis insists that what we are experiencing in relation to digital platforms and data extraction today really is part of a new, expanded colonial order.

We risk missing the significance of this new process entirely unless we connect two terms that until now have been largely unconnected: *data* and *colonialism*. This connection begins to make sense after we consider three initial propositions.

First, there can be no capitalism without colonialism. This is the reason why frameworks that try to make sense of what is happening with data exclusively in terms of the dynamics of post-industrial capitalism are not enough. There is a lot that is useful in those analyses,[2] but one crucial thing is missing: they ignore how capitalism itself only makes full sense against the background of colonialism. In other words, capitalism was only possible because of the vast wealth generated by the colonial land grab. Although capitalism has developed into a powerful global social system that binds human beings into particular modes of economic production for the benefit of elites, the system has always been connected (since its industrial phase) with a much larger arrangement that distributed labor and wealth in very unequal ways across the planet—for example, colonialism. Capitalism was, from the very start, part of a larger system that was colonial at its roots. Data colonialism merely represents the continuation of these dynamics, with data taking the place of land, labor or natural resources. The current system is not just about the *production* of new resources, but their *extraction* in a way that is characterized by injustice and dispossession.

Second, we must acknowledge that if capitalism and colonialism are intertwined in the manner just described, this must mean that colonialism is still evolving and that data colonialism is its latest stage. This point must be made carefully, since we are not suggesting that colonialism is immutable. On the contrary, we must pay careful attention to the similarities and differences between data colonialism and colonialism's earlier, more familiar stages.

We can explain this by separating out the form, content and function of colonialism. Because colonialism is a very complex historical process that has developed over centuries, its form and content have shifted and adapted with the times. By *form*, we mean the social and economic features of colonialism at any one time. Think, for instance, of how planter colonialism (grabbing land to grow cash crops) was very different from settler colonialism (appropriating land to live on it). By *content*, we mean the specific ways in which form manifested itself in different places and times. Think of how colonialism in Mexico by the Spaniards looked very different from colonialism in India by the British, which is, in turn, very different from data colonialism.

But there is one important similarity, one thing that all these forms of colonialism have in common. And that is the *function* of colonialism. The essential purpose of all types of colonialism is to extract, to dispossess. Colonialism always and everywhere means dispossessing others of what is theirs and taking it regardless of their rights. Whatever the nationality of the colonizer, whatever the geographical location or time period, colonialism has always been about colonizers taking something that does not belong to them through the use of power and deception. What is being colonized today is *human life itself*, and this is achieved through the extraction and capture of small fragments of our everyday existence in the form of data.

Finally, and following from all this, the third proposition that can help us understand how data and colonialism are linked is the idea that although digital data is a relatively new technology, it can—or rather, it must—be understood in the context of a 500-year planetary history of exploitation, not just as the outcome of the last 50 years of the so-called Information Revolution.

To understand this last point, we can take a quick look at the history of "cheap," starting with cheap nature. In order to colonize the world, nature had to be rendered cheap. Colonizers argued that the land and natural resources they took were abundant, free and just there for the taking. There was a whole "new" world awaiting the colonizer, whose arrival was often sufficient to justify a declaration that the new territories were his and his alone. An old legal doctrine was conveniently revived to make sense of this: the land taken was said to be without owner (*terra nullius* in Latin, which literally means No Man's Land; c.f. Cohen, 2018).

As we know, some of those territories had people living in them. But from the perspective of the colonizer, those people had no rights to the land, in part because they weren't using it to its full capacity (as defined by Western terms, of course). Because the colonizers could be relied upon to make the land more productive, they had an overriding right—so it was claimed—to take the land and do what they wanted with it. This is the backstory, for example, of how Western powers came to be in possession of the world's oil and much else besides.

In order to put that nature to good use, the colonizer needed another "cheap" resource: human labor. In historical colonialism, this labor was assumed by the colonizer to be free or almost free—just like cheap nature. Not everyone did that work: a pattern quickly emerged in who did what labor, a pattern mostly determined by race. This meant that local labor in the colonies was there for the taking: it came at a low cost, at least if you excluded the costs of the violence that held it under control. And so cheap labor transformed cheap nature into wealth.

Looking along the timeline of colonialism, we see a transition from cheap nature to cheap labor to, now . . . *cheap data*. Cheap data represents the same extractive rationality that we saw with cheap nature and cheap labor. Think of how much data we generate through our activities online: uploading and tagging content, liking posts, engaging in e-commerce, sharing things, being tracked as we move about the online and physical worlds. But to the platforms, all of this data arrives absolutely free. Data is said to be abundant, without owner and just there for the taking. Yes, you and I might produce it individually, but by the time it is aggregated and processed (data needs technologically intensive refining, much like other colonial resources), it is considered an ownerless exhaust or byproduct, and we can no longer exercise any claims to it. Our only job is thus to generate the resource, which we do just by carrying on our social life online. We are told this is what progress looks like, connecting us better and building better communities, communities that we are asked to imagine couldn't have been built any other way. But the real beneficiaries are the owners of the platforms and algorithmic processes that extract this data in order to generate profit.

An Internal Critique of Data Colonialism

Having laid out the major precepts of the data colonialism thesis, let us begin an internal critique of the argument.

To start with, we can ask whether important differences between colonialism and capitalism are being erased in this thesis. After all, colonialism and capitalism represent distinct social orders, and we cannot neatly equate the two. Rather than attempting to establish an equivalency, Couldry and I are trying to describe a new form of understanding the *relationship* between colonialism and capitalism. But how do we put two distinct historical periods in conversation with each other? In other words, what is the method, the historiography?

Another way of getting to this question is to ask whether the data colonialism thesis attempts to establish too much continuity. Identifying a similarity in *function* while minimizing differences in *form and content* allows us to establish a connection. Just as there was a continuity between planter colonialism and industrial capitalism, in that the wealth generated by the plantations financed the factories, the extraction of data from our lives is also generating a new reservoir of wealth that will be used to finance the next stage of capitalism.

Nonetheless, drawing a straight 500-year-long line from stolen land to stolen data asks us to collapse very complicated histories and processes. Tracing continuities between two very different historical moments is risky and prone to methodological missteps. To deepen the internal critique of data colonialism along these lines, it is useful to look at the work of Frederick Cooper (2005) and what we might call his *Four Deadly Sins of Vaguely Specified Temporalities*.

Cooper argues that despite a renaissance in scholarship about colonialism, the problem is that many authors (mostly non-historians) rely on a very generic conceptualization of colonialism: it started in 1492, ended sometime in the 1960s–1970s, and everything in between can be understood under the same rubric. The point of invoking colonialism in such a shorthanded way is to condemn exploitation and celebrate hybridity. These are not necessarily bad things, but what do we lose in the process?

Cooper identifies four specific methodological shortcomings (2005, pp. 17–22). To some extent, they can all be found within the data colonialism thesis. Let us consider, for instance, what these might look like in the context of the comparison we conduct in our work of the Spanish Requerimiento (the document read to indigenous peoples before colonizing them) and Google Chrome's Terms of Service or TOS (c.f. Couldry & Mejias, 2019, p. 92).

- *Story Plucking*: Taking a text or narrative (like the Requerimiento) and comparing it to other texts and narratives (like Chrome's TOS) at other times in history because, it is believed, there is a generic *essence* to being colonized, independent of historical differences.
- *Leapfrogging Legacies*: Starting at historical Point A (e.g., Requerimiento, 1513) and explaining what is happening at Point B (Google Chrome's Terms of Service from circa 2007) by collapsing 500 years of history.
- *Doing History Backward*: "confusing the analytic categories of the present with the native categories of the past" (Cooper, 2005, p. 18). For instance, thinking that the dispossession carried out by Google is similar to the dispossession carried out by the Spanish conquistadors.
- *The Epochal Fallacy*: Forgetting that the colonial and postcolonial periods are not coherent wholes, although sometimes they are discussed as such. History is not demarcated by epochal periods with neat beginnings, middles and ends.

The reason these historiographical transgressions matter, according to Cooper, is because history as an inevitability obscures politics; or, to put it differently, ahistorical history results in apolitical politics (2005, p. 25). Context and specificity matter, and to engage in the kind of transhistorical analysis that argues that because one thing happened in context/time X, a similar thing is inevitably happening in context/time Y can obscure the power arrangements of context/time Y and prevent us from understanding it fully.

In that sense, some pertinent critiques have been made of the data colonialism thesis. We have been asked, for instance, whether we are suggesting that colonialism looked the same in Brazil as it did in Indonesia and whether we think *data* colonialism looks the same today in those same locations. We have also been asked about the ways in which issues of class, gender and race make each instance of data colonialism unique and specific, to the extent that subsuming all those differences under one label might prevent us from understanding the politics of each context (I will say more about class, gender and race subsequently). While these observations are valid, Couldry and

I have been more interested in constructing a broad theoretical framework for understanding what is happening with data globally rather than analyzing specific case studies and their intersectionality (the kind of case study that would allow us to say something specific about, say, black women gig workers in Brazil). Furthermore, I would argue that there is actually some value in the story plucking and leapfrogging we have done, which I will attempt to explain next.

Colonialism and Big Science

It should be clear to most readers that *The Costs of Connection* (Couldry & Mejias, 2019) is not a history book. Examples were "plucked" based on their potential to explain why the large-scale extraction of a resource that seems cheap—but that isn't—is not without precedent. Doing history and doing critical studies of technology are two separate endeavors with different goals. Doing history is important to keep a rich record not just of facts but of the interpretation of those facts at different moments. But doing critical theory means using history for the purpose of constructing a present that will allow us to imagine a different future, even if it means taking some historiographical liberties.

In other words, *doing history backward*, which Cooper decries, can be a good way of *doing history forward*. Historians should try to avoid the methodological shortcomings Cooper has identified. But Cooper himself acknowledges that understanding the complexities of the colonial past in detail should help us broaden "our sense of the opportunities and constraints of the future" (2005, p. 32). So even for Cooper, understanding the past is a way of acting in the present and future. As such, for non-historians trying to achieve social change, historical detail is important insofar as it allows them to mobilize social actors (not only for positive but also for negative ends, it should be noted). Put differently, to explain the present, historical accuracy must often be subordinated to the opportunity to enact change. Although it sounds unscholarly, this way of *doing history forward* is what most of us do with history: selectively aligning lessons from the past to create new meanings out of the present.

To demonstrate, I would like to engage in more of this faulty historiography to connect extraction, science, data, profit and computing all under the vaguely specified temporality of colonialism. My excuse for engaging in this form of story plucking is to create a way to intervene in the present to change the way we think about the future.

Soon after the plunder of the Americas began, the Spanish Crown formed an administrative bureau called the Casa de la Contratación de las Indias, which was charged with the task of setting up an accounting system for all the gold, silver and other precious materials being extracted and shipped to the Old World. It is estimated that more than 181 tons of gold and 16,000 tons of silver flowed from America to Spain between 1500 and 1650 (Benjamin, 2006).

Keeping track of this wealth was a challenge, which the Spaniards addressed by recording it in books called "libros de cargo y data," using a double entry accounting system (Donoso Anes, 2012). Obviously, the word "data" here means something different than what it means to us now, which is why we must try to avoid "confusing the analytic categories of the present with the native categories of the past," as Cooper says (2005). And yet, we can see the libros de cargo y data, along with other technologies and tools, as important innovations in colonial administration.

Plucking these examples is important because it allows us to frame scientific and technological evolution (which includes the evolution of management tools) as part of a problem of administrating extracted resources, from colonialism to today. To help us make sense of this evolution, we can think about the fact that, as Claude Alvares (1988) points out, the Scientific Method (at least in a form we would recognize) and what we might call the Colonizing Method emerged around the same time and evolved together. This is not a coincidence. According to Alvares, "science and technology are both colonizing activities, [and] any suggestions about delinking them from imperialism can only be fraudulent" (1988, p. 73). In summary, Alvares' argument is that the scientific method and the application of science as a whole are peculiar forms of Western madness that destroy nature and humanity and eliminate diversity—all in the process of extracting resources for the generation of wealth. In Alvares' view, modern science and colonialism share deep historical links because they are, in fact, the same project, that is, conquering the world in the name of, and for, one group of people. In order to accomplish this complicated managerial task, Western/colonial science relies on a crucial tool: abstraction.

In the scientific laboratory, everything that does not contribute to the goal of managing resources is put aside or eliminated to generate an "objective" view of the subject. This process of abstraction is used by Western science to classify and control the thing being studied. After eliminating what is considered irrelevant, what remains is an object open to manipulation and exploitation. Data is an important element in this process of abstraction since it reduces natural and social elements to a form of knowledge that can be used to manage the world. The more data science has about something, the purer the abstraction and the more opportunities for manipulation.

From this perspective, computer science (including AI) emerges as a continuation of the colonial impulse to govern the world. Data makes us and the world manageable. For example, data captured about my facial expression at a given time can be used by corporations or states to infer my mood and classify me in a particular way (to sell me things as a consumer or make certain assumptions about me as a citizen). Since the data about my facial expression is extracted or mined, not given (despite what the legal agreements might have us believe), there is justification to call this not just a capitalist but a colonialist order.

If we follow this premise, it is not necessarily remarkable that the structures for maintaining a social order that revolves around data extraction emerged so quickly in the 50–70 years of the Digital Revolution. These structures seem to have emerged rapidly, but they are in fact firmly rooted in processes that are much older and well established. As we began to see in the earlier discussion of cheap data, they did not need to be invented from scratch. By engaging in a bit of *doing history backward*, we can see that the foundations for something resembling Big Tech and Big Science began to emerge during colonialism, as I describe next.

According to Steven Harris (2011), the operation of long-distance corporations during colonialism required substantial investments in science. Enterprises such as the Casa de la Contratación de las Indias (in Spain) or the East India Company (in England) were tasked with managing colonies remotely, across great distances. New tools had to be developed by scientists and inventors employed by these corporations to make this possible. But who were these scientists?

While cultural myths encourage us to think of science as the sum of contributions from individual geniuses (Galileo, Bacon, Newton, etc.), Harris makes the case that colonialism introduced a kind of Big Science that had just as much impact as that of the scientific celebrities but that gets a lot less attention. This Big Science was done by large groups of people all over the world, acting in concert for the benefit of their corporate employers.

> By the end of the seventeenth century, most of the big sciences [observational astronomy, geography, natural history, meteorology, navigation, etc.] could claim to be cumulative enterprises with ever-increasing stores of treatises, manuals, tables, maps, charts, reports, handbooks, globes (both celestial and terrestrial), instruments, and specimens.
>
> (Harris, p. 79)

In other words, colonial expansion and management were carried out through global corporations (Big Tech) employing hundreds of scientists (Big Science) who developed the intellectual and technological structures required for the political, military and cultural subjugation of the world. Furthermore, this required the collection and analysis of vast amounts of information from the colonies (Big Data) in the form of maps, surveys, libros de cargo y data, and so on. And the singular purpose of much of this information was the surveillance and control (Big Brother) of the colonized people. Not for nothing were tools like passports and technologies like fingerprinting invented in the colonies and then imported to the center of the empire (c.f. Sodhi & Kaur, 2005).

Thus, I would go as far as saying that colonialism, not the Digital Revolution, is the origin point for the convergence of Big Tech, Big Science, Big Data and Big Brother. Put differently, it was the cumulative inventions of Big Science that allowed Big Tech to use Big Data to act as Big Brother—and all of this was already unfolding 500 years ago, long before GAFA (Google, Apple, Facebook and Amazon), BATX (Baidu, Alibaba, Tencent and Xiaomi) and the rest of the players making up the "social quantification sector" (Couldry & Mejias, 2018, 2019).

This amount of *doing history backward* would probably worry Cooper greatly. But my hope is that this exercise can also help us *do history forward* in a critical way, to which I turn next.

The Coloniality of Data Classes

Colonial science was in large part about classification. When we stroll through the beautiful botanical gardens of European cities, for example, we are essentially walking through data centers that categorized and ordered knowledge about plants imported from the Global South. But there were other more egregious examples of colonial classification, such as scientific racism, which tried to rationalize the superiority of white men vis-à-vis people of color (and white women too) on pseudo-biological and anthropological terms.

One of the most pervasive categorization schemes developed during colonialism (and extended through capitalism) is the idea of society itself. The Peruvian sociologist Aníbal Quijano argued that "there is no such thing that we can call 'society' that really exists" (2000, p. 9). In his analysis, the idea of the social as a unified totality needs to be rejected as an attempt to exert a colonial logic to control the assumed parts of a whole.

> [T]he idea of totality is not only unnecessary, but is above all an epistemological distortion. . . . Eurocentrism has led virtually the whole world to accept the idea that within a totality, the whole has absolute determinant primacy over all of the parts, and that therefore there is one and only one logic that governs the behavior of the whole and all of the parts.
>
> (Quijano, 2000, pp. 8–9)

In that sense, I would argue that data is an expression of coloniality, because it integrates disparate entities into a totality that can be managed. Consider, for instance, the Facebook profile. It can accommodate all variants of humans; in fact, the more diverse and heterogenous the people who create the profiles, the better. The platform can standardize and templatize such differences to create a platform that is capable of containing and classifying all that difference (and, in turn, extracting data from and targeting advertisements to these classes of individuals).

According to Quijano, colonialism developed three interconnected classification schema (what today we could perhaps call *data classes*) that were instrumental in creating the illusion that human differences could only be reconciled through a universalizing Western rationality. Those three schema were race, gender and class. Through them, colonial logic (and capitalist logic, subsequently) built a social order that could be controlled and dominated. In this context, it is possible to see identity politics as a legacy of colonialism, a system of separation and classification that facilitates the exercise of colonial and capitalist power. Claiming my identity (checking the appropriate boxes during the creation of my social media profile) is an act of finding others like me and differentiating myself antagonistically from others unlike me: men against women, white against black, rich against poor . . . and all possible intersections in between. With all that difference in circulation, it is only the fiction of the whole (first a society, now a digital platform) that can hold us together. But that fiction is being narrated by "one and only one logic that governs the behavior of the whole and of the parts," as Quijano says (2000, p. 9). Thus, Western logic is imposed on the rest of the world, posing as universal.

This means that data do not facilitate control by eliminating difference, but by exploiting difference, exploiting both in the sense of generating more and more difference that can be managed (through the creation of more and more variated data sub-classes) and in the sense of commodifying or commercializing difference (for instance, by creating more and more opportunities to target content and advertisement to specific sub-classes). Difference—in the form of hyper-specific data classes—can be used to exaggerate divisions among us, diverting blame from the colonizers to their victims, who are told they do not have to get along with those who are different because the platform can help them find those who are the same. The colonizer presents the illusion of the platform as the only social whole capable of managing all this difference.

Because the system is built around the data categories of class, gender and race, it is also these data classes that must serve as analytical frameworks to critique and dismantle the system. In other words, class, gender and race (and their intersections) can still provide useful frameworks to understand the structure of the system. At the same time, class, gender and race must be superseded as models of political action. We must stop using them as the building blocks of an unsustainable social whole. But what shall we use instead of an identity model based on race, class and gender?

Decolonizing and Declassifying Data

It is possible to imagine data as a non-extractive resource, one capable of creating both difference and totality without using a colonizing model. What is presented here are only some preliminary notes on how to begin to do this, based on my earlier work on nodocentrism and paranodality (Mejias, 2013).

Nodocentrism is the network's internal logic that organizes and renders the world in terms of nodes, to the exclusion of anything that is not a node. In describing the relationship that nodes have to things internal and external to the network, Manuel Castells writes:

> The topology defined by networks determines that the distance (or intensity and frequency of interaction) between two points (or social positions) is shorter (or more frequent, or more intense) if both points are nodes in a network than if they do not belong to the same network. On the other hand, within a given network, flows have no distance, or the same distance, between nodes. Thus, distance (physical, social, economic, political, cultural) for a given point or position varies between zero (for any node in the same network) and infinite (for any point external to the network).
>
> (Castells, 2000, p. 501)

In other words, whereas the distance between two nodes that are part of the same network is finite, the distance between something inside the network and something outside the network is *infinite* (even if, in spatial terms, that distance is quite short). Nodocentrism means that while networks are extremely efficient at establishing links between nodes, they embody a bias against knowledge of—and engagement with—anything that is not a node in the same network.

That is why if I'm looking for restaurants on Google Maps in the city I'm visiting, and a restaurant is not indexed by Google, it might as well not exist. The point is not that nodocentrism in digital networks impoverishes social life or devalues what is around us: nodes behave neither anti-socially (they thrive in linking to other nodes) nor anti-locally (they can link to other nodes in their immediate surroundings just as easily as they can link to remote nodes). The point, rather, is that nodocentrism constructs a social reality in which nodes can only see other nodes. The network is an episteme, a way to make sense of reality, and nodocentrism is a form of epistemological exclusivity that renders the world only in terms of nodes. Only nodes can be mapped, explained, or accounted for.

Nodocentrism does not provide an inadequate picture of the world, just an incomplete one. It rationalizes a model of progress and development where those elements that are outside the network can only acquire currency by becoming part of the network. This is a colonialist logic. *Bridging the digital divide* is normalized as an end across societies that wish to partake of the benefits of modernity. The assumption behind the discourse of the digital divide is that one side, technologically advanced and accomplished societies must help the other side (technologically underdeveloped or retarded) catch up. Network logic thus motivates us to bring inside what is outside, which, of course, entails a colonial politics of inclusion and exclusion.

But let's shift our attention now away from the nodes. Imagine a network map, with its usual nodes and links. Now, shift your attention away from the nodes to the negative space between them. In network diagrams, the space around a node is rendered in perfect emptiness, stillness and silence. Far from being empty or barren, this is the domain of the paranodal, the space inhabited by what does not conform to the organizing logic of the network.

Only the paranodal can suggest alternatives that exist beyond the exclusivity of nodes. Digital networks and their data classes create new templates for organizing sociality, but it is only by going beyond the logic of the network that differences from established social norms can be claimed. The paranodal is a site for correcting the nodocentrism that reduces difference to class, gender and race. It is the launching pad for social desires that cannot be contained by these categories. The node, with its static identity and a predefined place and purpose within the network, dissolves into something that can occupy other forms of difference.

The paranodal might be, to use Rancière's terminology, *the part of those who have no part* (1999, p. 9). But the paranodal is not passive or subordinate; it has as much power in defining space and relations as the nodes in the network. That is the reason paranodal space is so important—the peripheries of the nodes represent the only sites from which it is possible to unthink or disidentify from the network. Social progress (new identities, new actions) requires experimentation, and the paranodal allows for deviation from the prevailing norms of network logic.

Which is why decolonizing data must be approached as a creative form of resistance, not from the outside of the network but from its internal paranodal spaces. The paranodal can shape the network in very powerful ways, focusing the attention of nodes on the limits of the dataset classes used to structure their reality. In other words, we must help nodes see their nodocentrism for what it is: a form of colonial extractivism that feeds on our social lives, a classification scheme that uses class, gender and race to create differences that can be controlled, and a totality not worth subscribing to because it only produces injustice and inequality. As we stand at the paranodal borders of the network, we can imagine a new whole that does not exploit its parts.

Doing History Backward and Forward

At the risk of oversimplifying the issue, we could think of the present as a *whole* and the past and the future as constituted of *parts*. The reverse could also be true, of course, but for the sake of the argument, this is what I mean: our extractivist present is presented to us as a complete reality, a here-and-now over which we have little control. There is no escaping this present, especially when it is presented to us as progress, as something that takes cheap inputs and "efficiently" transforms them into valuable and convenient outputs without much consideration for the externalized costs. The past and the future, on the other hand, can always be reinterpreted and reimagined. New memories, new links, new facts and understandings add to an assemblage of parts that, unlike the present, cannot be contained, helping us build more complicated pictures of our yesterdays and tomorrows.

When looking at the present, we see that colonial and capitalist structures are extremely resilient and resistant; their extractivism stretches not only across vast geographies but also across latent temporalities, colonizing/totalizing potential pasts and futures. Data colonialism invades our present imagination and limits our ability to think of alternatives. It attempts to sell us a single present that ignores the fact that the past and the future are plural and polysemic, made up of many parts. This totalizing present appears indestructible, unchangeable.

We must always remember that even if the present seems determined, the past and the future are always open to revision, and their parts are always mutable. Decolonizing the whole/present through its parts/pasts, its nodes through its paranodes, requires radical decolonial historiographies. One concrete and practical thing we can do as part of this process of decolonizing data is to rewrite the history of computer science to account for its extractive and colonialist role while also rescuing its democratizing tendencies where appropriate. By doing that, we can expose the classification schemes data has constructed to control us: class, gender and race, and their endless intersections. These dataset classes have created the illusion of diversity while allowing those who control the platforms to retain control over the whole/present. In that sense, doing history *backward* and *forward* is a good antidote to data colonialism, because it creates more parts. It counters narratives about universalizing totalities and immutable presents with narratives about subversive parts that can shape the present and the future, opening the way to imagining new unquantifiable wholes helping us see the possibilities that emerge when we stand at the edges of the network.

Notes

1 Thanks to the organizers of the symposium—Jonnie Penn, Matthew L. Jones, Richard Staley, Sarah Dillon, Stephanie A. Dick and Syed Mustafa Ali—for inviting me to share my thoughts. Thanks also to Asma Barlas, Hunter Heyck and Nick Couldry for their comments on the lecture. The overview of the data colonialism thesis relies heavily on work done in collaboration with Nick.
2 See, for instance, the theories of digital capitalism (Schiller, 1999), platform capitalism (Srnicek, 2016), data capitalism (Mayer-Schoenberger and Ramke, 2018), informational capitalism (Cohen, 2019) and surveillance capitalism (Zuboff, 2019).

References

Alvares, C. (1988). Science, colonialism and violence: A luddite view. In A. Nandy (Ed.), *Science, hegemony and violence: A requiem for modernity*. Oxford University Press. https://archive.unu.edu/unupress/unupbooks/uu05se/uu05se07.htm
Benjamin, T. (Ed.). (2006). *Encyclopedia of Western colonialism since 1450*. Macmillan Reference.

Castells, M. (2000). *The rise of the network society* (2nd ed.). Blackwell Publishers.

Cohen, J. E. (2018). The biopolitical public domain: The legal construction of the surveillance economy. *Philosophy & Technology, 31*, 213–233. https://doi.org/10.1007/s13347-017-0258-2

Cohen, J. E. (2019). *Between truth and power: The legal constructions of informational capitalism.* Oxford University Press. https://doi.org/10.1093/oso/9780190246693.001.0001

Collingwood, R. G. (1933). *An essay on philosophical method.* Oxford University Press.

Cooper, F. (2005). *Colonialism in question: Theory, knowledge, history.* University of California Press.

Couldry, N., & Mejias, U. A. (2018). Data colonialism: Rethinking big data's relation to the contemporary subject. *Television & New Media.* https://doi.org/10.1177/1527476418796632

Couldry, N., & Mejias, U. A. (2019). *The costs of connection: How data is colonizing human life and appropriating it for capitalism.* Stanford University Press.

Couldry, N., & Mejias, U. A. (2021). The decolonial turn in data and technology research: What is at stake and where is it heading? *Information, Communication & Society,* 1–17. https://doi.org/10.1080/1369118X.2021.1986102

Donoso Anes, R. (2012). La documentación contable de la Tesorería de la Casa de la Contratación de las Indias de Sevilla (1503–1717). *Comptabilités, 3.* http://journals.openedition.org/comptabilites/754

Harris, S. J. (2011). Long-distance corporations, big sciences, and the geography of knowledge. In S. Harding (Ed.), *The postcolonial science and technology studies reader* (pp. 61–83). Duke University Press Books.

Mayer-Schönberger, V., & Ramge, T. (2018). *Reinventing capitalism in the age of big data.* Basic Books.

Mejias, U. A. (2013). *Off the Network: Disrupting the Digital World.* University of Minnesota Press.

Quijano, A. (2000). Colonialidad del Poder y Clasificación Social. *Journal of World-Systems Research, 6*(2), 342–386.

Rancière, J. (1999). *Disagreement: Politics and philosophy.* University of Minnesota Press.

Schiller, D. (1999). *Digital capitalism: Networking the global market system.* MIT Press.

Sodhi, G. S., & Kaur, J. (2005). The forgotten Indian pioneers of fingerprint science. *Current Science, 88*(1), 185–191.

Srnicek, N. (2016). *Platform capitalism.* Polity.

Zuboff, P. S. (2019). *The age of surveillance capitalism: The fight for a human future at the new frontier of power.* Profile Books.

2 Metadata Is Not Data About Data

Kyle Parry

Do a search for the term "metadata" in the early 2020s, and you'll find that one definition continues to enjoy pride of place: "data about data." The idea is relatively simple. Metadata refers to a special type of data. What distinguishes this type of data is neither its mode (such as qualitative or quantitative) nor its status (such as raw or processed), but its role. Whether as URLs, subject headings, tags, or still other creations, instances of metadata stand in a secondary relationship to other data. They are data that describe or document things of concern, whether that means the provenance of a data set on sea levels, the timing of a readout from a distant probe or the geolocation of a customer. If there are debates in the world of metadata, then they should—according to this line of thinking anyway—center on tools and structures for managing objects and information.

As dominant as this way of looking at metadata has become, it's not the only one that's out there. In fact, what we might think of as the landscape of metadata conceptualizations is both varied and evolving. True enough that a very large subset of that landscape takes as given what I have just summarized: the idea that the now six-decade-old term "metadata" essentially refers to data that describes other data. And yet, if you take the time to read across these literatures, you won't just find nuanced adjustments to that core notion, such as the adoption of variations on "information about a resource" within certain sectors of the International Organization for Standardization (Furner, 2020, p. E35). You'll also find statements of opposition. Few in number, but compelling in their reasoning, these statements contend that "data about data" is a recipe for limited thinking about a consequential phenomenon. Some even suggest that the flaws in this definition are reflective of flaws in the very idea of metadata itself: that metadata is not really the consistent and widespread thing different fields make it out to be, and that therefore we ought to use the term only sparingly or even jettison it entirely.

In surveying these different conceptions of metadata, we can try to decide which is the most convincing and therefore should become the standard, but we can also venture into more uncertain terrain. We can be unconvinced by the options and, just as significantly, by the idea of picking just one. The

DOI: 10.4324/9781003299912-2

assumption would be that, with the rise of social media and widespread, automated surveillance, and in further consideration of enduring calls to contest and to decolonize only seemingly natural terms of debate, the time has come to rethink our approach to the many materials and practices that fall under the umbrella of "metadata." This would be a practice of critical and expansive, but not total and final, reconceptualization. Existing critiques of "data about data" would not be overcome or denied; they would be treated as resources and provocations for an underexplored line of inquiry that takes metadata's definitional uncertainty as a difficult but ultimately tractable given. The goal would not be indefinite conceptual play, nor would it be a definitive conceptual conclusion. It would be more flexible and more effective and even more just conceptions of these typically structured, typically machine-readable meta materials that append and infuse (and sometimes themselves become) what is considered primary. In short, we can ask: if metadata isn't—or isn't just—data about data, then what else is it and why should we care?

Misleading, Restrictive and Imprecise

It's difficult to precisely place when the phrase "data about data" began to circulate, but critiques of the notion appear to be relatively recent, potentially a reflection of the increasing scope and sophistication (and skepticism) in debates on metadata. Three versions of this critique are especially noteworthy.

One appears in Jeffrey Pomerantz's widely cited *Metadata*. Early in the text, Pomerantz argues that the popular definition, while "catchy," is the "least useful" (2015, p. 19). One problem is the term "data." For Pomerantz (2015, p. 26), "data is only potential information, raw and unprocessed, prior to anyone actually being informed by it"; in other words, "data" establishes the wrong conceptual frame for metadata, because it is, in his mind, informing and being informed that really are at issue. The other problem is the word "about." Referring to subject analysis (the labor of classifying what given texts concern), Pomerantz emphasizes that "determining what something is about is subjective"; it requires not only "an understanding of that thing" but also of the "available terms" through which one can describe that thing. From Pomerantz's perspective, the phrase "about data" fails to capture this interpretive complexity.

Despite these doubts, Pomerantz ends up arguing that data about data can be "salvaged." The key, he contends, is to shift our perspective. When we are talking about things like keywords, ID numbers and instructions for preservation, we are talking about a class of objects in the world with the distinct quality of being potentially informative with respect to other objects, of possibly telling us something we need or want to know about these other objects, whether for the purposes of finding, storing or otherwise. From this vantage, metadata is newly conceived as "a potentially informative object" that characteristically "describes another potentially informative object." Or, in Pomerantz's subsequent and self-consciously less "clunky" version, metadata is "a statement about a potentially informative object"; for example, the presence of the name Leonardo da Vinci in a "creator" field associated with *Mona Lisa* amounts to a "potentially informative" statement that someone of this name created the painting (and, at least from this informational point of view, the painting is likewise "potentially informative").

For a second version of the critique of "data about data," the popular phrase isn't so much misleading as restrictive. For Ranger (2012), for instance, metadata is definitely "information about an object," but it is also information about how you can find that object "in a messy file structure," and it is information about how you can or ought to use that object; it is data about the use of data. For Koster (2015), the situation is more fraught. Metadata can be data about data, but this is only the case in some rather than all situations; consequently, the term is "confusing," even "superfluous." If we were to try to isolate the phenomenon, then we would have to recognize the many other things that count as metadata, from information about "virtual entities, physical objects [and] information contained in these objects" to information about "events, concepts [and] people." In other words, there is an inertia in the landscape of metadata conceptualizations, such that the memorable aphorism "data about data" serves to undermine attention to the considerable reach of the phenomenon, a reach that extends well into social, material and historical worlds. Metadata doesn't just refer to data and objects; it also refers to actions, histories and economies—to the lives and deaths of people, places and institutions.

The last significant line of criticism I'll cite is less about what the phrase "data about data" leaves out and more about its imprecision relative to real-world examples. In a 1977 US government manual on information management, for instance, the authors qualify their recommendations with this warning:

> It would have been awkward, and in some cases, almost impossible, to label each reference of information as to whether we were talking about substantive information or whether we were talking about metadata. The reader should, in the context of the discussion, determine which of these two types we are talking about, if, in fact, we are not talking about *both* substantive information and metadata.
>
> (Commission on Federal Paperwork, 1977, p. v, emphasis in original)

In the eyes of some later critics, this difficulty in drawing the line between data and metadata—between the "substantive" and the secondary, the content and the context—is more than reason for caution; it is reason for near-total abandonment. Few state the case as clearly as open data activist Michael Kreil (Exposing the Invisible, 2016):

> I have a problem with the term "metadata." I don't think that this term is precise, because, simply put, the basic idea of metadata is that it's data about data. For example, if I take a photo, I can add data like the camera model, time and geolocation, so, the additional information about when and where the photo was shot is called metadata. But, for example, if I take a lot of photos, I can use the metadata contained in these photos to connect the location in which I took them with the time I took them. The metadata can be used to track me. So, from that point of view, metadata is the data itself, and that's the interesting aspect, not the photos themselves.

For Kreil (and it's important to note he's not alone in this sentiment), the upshot of the term's imprecision is not a recognition that the prevailing conception of metadata is too limited. It is a recognition that metadata is rarely just metadata and that, therefore, the use of the term should be quite restricted. "In general, from a public point of view," Kreil clarifies, "everything is data, which is usually about persons. So let's stop calling it metadata." If some people continue to call things metadata, these should only be people who "add data to the data."

Fluid, Multiple, Fractional and Non-neutral

"Data about data" is the most efficient and inclusive definition of metadata; it is misleading; it is restrictive; and it is imprecise. Taking stock of these four takes on the dominant definition (and surely there are others), we find ourselves at a conceptual crossroads.

At first blush, it seems reasonable to take the path that has become familiar, the one that accords with prevailing cultures of metadata and that is arguably implicit in each of the arguments here. We assess which string of words can serve as the best possible standard definition, the one that will hold up for a variety of users across a variety of contexts, a definition that can encompass the "complex technical and intellectual infrastructure to manage and retrieve digital objects in different digital contexts, within different digital information systems and services" (Méndez & van Hooland, 2014). We can ask: Is it better to open the concept of metadata to a wider set of objects, or is it better to keep things quite restricted, as Kreil suggests? If it is better to open things up, is the Pomerantz emphasis on informative statements the most effective and inclusive, or is even that approach beset by problems of restriction and bias, erroneously assuming it's all about information and underplaying metadata's social and material entanglements? Would it make more sense to accept the aphorism and then develop more precise definitions for specific fields? Or should we just forget the whole business of questioning core concepts of metadata, as though this was a case of solutions in search of problems?

As compelling as these questions are, they prove unreliable when subjected to more critically and historically intensive scrutiny. It's convenient to treat metadata as a "definite and singular" concept, to use Matthew Mayernik's helpful framing (2020). One assumes that when Philip R. Bagley (apparently) coined the term in the 1960s, he succeeded in identifying a new element within the world of data and information; that element would grow and proliferate, but the core structure—something like data or information that describes other data or information—would remain the same. And yet this isn't what happened. For one thing, as Koster's insistence on the social and material reach of metadata suggests, there has been a significant increase in the variety of metadata types. Mayernik notes that metadata are as varied as "file naming conventions, catalog records, data descriptions in repositories, user tags on YouTube, notes in personal Excel spreadsheets, email headers, and HTML tags." To this list we must add further varieties in the realm of "user tags": forms of metadata that involve the passions and perspectives of everyday people, such as the hashtags that serve as the slogans and calling cards of social movements. We can also add more than types. Mayernik notes that people perform metadata "differently in different social settings and situations." They enact metadata as "Dublin Core records created by information professionals"; they enact it as "descriptions in lab notebooks created by scientists to document their data"; or (I would add) they put them into practice as part of the language of social media, as with the slew of metadata elements that have become second nature to those who frequent platforms like TikTok: the likes, hashtags, timestamps, usernames and even the textual labels overlaid onto videos, the ingredients of a media practice I think of as "expressive folksonomy" (Parry, 2023).

At least one other development undermines the idea of metadata as enduringly definite and singular. It has become increasingly clear that metadata cannot be separated from economic and political domination. This is evident in the writings I've cited, as when Kreil refers to the uses of metadata as data for surveillance or when Pomerantz recalls the use of metadata as the basis for killings by the United States military, as voiced in former CIA and NSA director Michael Hayden's unforgettable admission, "We kill people based on metadata." Metadata's relationships to domination are also evident from other angles, such as recent projects in reparative and decolonial description and knowledge organization. Here there is a recognition that countless descriptive inheritances—terms, summaries, inventories and taxonomies—owe their origins and outlines to histories of racism and imperialism, and that conscious efforts must be made to assert other vocabularies, other understandings, other voices and other stakes, in however limited or imperfect a fashion (Adler, 2016; Frick & Proffitt, 2022). And this is just one among many power-conscious and justice-driven approaches to metadata. There are, for instance, the efforts of indigenous communities to contest only seemingly universal protocols like Dublin Core through Traditional Knowledge (TK) labels, as explored by María Montenegro (2019). There is also Thomas N. Cooke's reframing of the seeming marginality and banality of metadata as a smoke-screen, as with the "coalescing of mutual interests within the big data and smartphone manufacturing industries to maintain the invisibility and illegibility of metadata" (2020, p. 91)—metadata as a murky "mechanism of capital" (2020, p. 92), a kind of half-open, sociotechnical secret.

Taking all these developments into account, one can no longer treat a list of basic conceptions of metadata as a straightforward menu of options. Not only are we faced with a notion that didn't come fully formed—Bagley notably put the word "about" in quotation marks when introducing the neologism (Bagley, 1968, p. 26)—we also face a set of multiple, mutually compelling propositions with respect to how that term should now be defined, conceived and enacted, including the idea that the term should be effectively discarded in favor of full-fledged attention to data. We are also (or so one hopes) confronted with the need for both relative clarity on the objects of concern and a meaningful orientation toward the fraught and exploitative dimensions of the phenomenon as it exists and is put to use, no longer assuming that metadata is some neutral substrate or afterthought, instead heeding its evolving roles in practices of extraction and domination.

The question is what to do. My fundamental argument in this chapter is that the time has come to test new approaches. We can start by taking as given what Mayernik lays out: that metadata is not "definite and singular" but "fluid, multiple, and fractional," which is not to say it is infinitely redefinable but that it is marked by conceptions and sub-conceptions that are many, interconnected and at times contradictory. We can then add to this list of traits, asserting that the concept is also non-neutral; similar to how systems of classification "impose their own rationale" and assert a "way of seeing the world" (Montenegro, 2019, p. 737), conceptions of metadata favor certain ways of thinking, seeing and valuing over others. Having adopted these critical frames, we can then proceed on a path of creative skepticism. We can suggest that the conceptual landscape of metadata is insufficiently elaborated, and we can then ask what alternative definitions, categories and typologies will prove meaningful and useful. None of this would be done in the spirit of total correction because that would be out of step with the basic premise of metadata as a fluid, multiple, fractional and non-neutral concept. Rather, this would be done in the spirit of plurality and justice: metadata understood not from the perspective of orthodox objects like canonical paintings and commercial barcodes, but from the perspective of contrasting and contested practices, whether that's the exploitation of machine-learning assessed user characteristics or anticolonial tagging.

In short, to ask why and how metadata isn't (or isn't only) "data about data" is to see "Who's right?" in one direction and "What else?" in another.

Taking this latter path, we pose questions about metadata that combine the conceptual, the critical and the creative. What has been left out, overlooked, or overemphasized in conceptions of metadata, and how might these silences, absences and imbalances be meaningfully counteracted? Is there reason to abandon the concept altogether, as Koster and Kreil suggest, or is it possible to take a reparative or even radical approach to metadata?

Data Near Data

Of the many conceivable ways into this terrain, testing hidden premises is the one I am best positioned to attempt. What's something that is consistent across both the default and the corrective definitions that might yet be called into question? How might this consistent element be rethought with the help of fields not typically understood as concerned with metadata?

Most obviously, there are the consistent elements of data and information, but there is also that other term Pomerantz briefly addresses: "about." With the caveats that no definition is neutral and that aboutness remains to be theorized in depth, we can lean on the definition offered by Stephen Yablo (2014, p. 1) in an eponymous book: aboutness is "the relation that meaningful items bear to whatever it is that they are on or off or that they address or concern." To say that this relation is prevalent in the world of metadata would be an understatement. Not only did Bagley's framing of the term put aboutness front and center, saying that the type of data for which he didn't quite have a name could be thought of as data with the quality of being "about" other data, subsequent discussions of metadata in the world of libraries have often included discussions of the subject matter of texts, and subject matter is often the thing we speak to when we use this preposition (Holley & Joudrey, 2021).

Adding to the apparent appeal of aboutness, it seems to hold up quite well when applied to new metadata varieties. For instance, in adding a description like "the problem is capitalism" to an image of a factory floor posted to social media, a user would typically be indicating that the post is somehow related to, based on or from debates on political economy; the description tells us something about the post's subject matter. At the same time, another type of metadata that attends the post, the number of accumulated likes, is not an indication that the post concerns capitalism and other forms; it is a potentially informative statement about the status of the post in comparison to others. Whether or not users take the time to read these different metadata elements, they will find themselves confronted with multiple informational relations at the nexus of metadata and aboutness. That nexus isn't only significant for users; the post also serves as a convergence of tags, topics and usage data for businesses. For example, the fact that a user has taken time to pause and read the post could be treated as indicative, adding to the trove of data about them (and about those deemed to share their categories) and potentially altering the kinds of topics assumed to interest them for the next refreshes of their feeds and "for you" pages, even serving as avenues for their continued capture in loops of attention and extraction (Cooke, 2020). In other words, what is explicitly a post about (concerning, addressing) capitalism is also, structurally speaking, a post "about" (having to do with, turning on, relevant to, enmeshed within) surveillance capitalism (Zuboff, 2019).

Given these ways in which aboutness is not only quite ingrained but also persistently active and germane, it's clearly going to require some shaking up of our habits and assumptions to see anything else at work, and there's no guarantee that alternatives will be valuable. One thing we can do is zoom out to consider ideas and approaches from fields not traditionally concerned with metadata, such as visual studies and cultural theory. More importantly, we can do something this collection encourages and which I, as a scholar who tends to write about culture and media in the United States, am learning to do by way of unlearning: we can also look to writers who have been critiquing Western epistemologies for a long time. What these writers often do is refuse to take fundamental assumptions as givens, instead seeing that the concepts that dominate European and Anglo-American discourses come from particular places, produce oversights and serve particular purposes, including purposes of exploitation and domination (Smith, 2021). Crucially, these writers will not look at the prevalence and usefulness of a framework like aboutness as any assurance of an essential or universal status. Instead, as is already the case with a small set of contemporary artists, they will approach aboutness with attention to power relations. Aboutness can name the habit of fashioning a strict, stable argument or zeroing in on a relevant and topical subject matter (Berwald, 2016; Raina & Smith, 2018). It can be the posture of distanced description epitomized in imperial documentation of colonized peoples. Aboutness can even be reframed as a widely active construct that must undergo decolonization; it maintains the political, economic and ecological status quo even under the veneer of urgency (Ashbel, 2019; Wenner, 2021).

Especially useful along these lines is a critical gesture that many writers have cited, and that I've cited elsewhere as well. At some point in the development of her 1982 film *Reassemblage*, Trinh T. Minh-ha determined that the dominant, aboutness-centered way of thinking about the project wasn't appropriate. One might think that a film made up of footage of women's lives in rural Senegal would be a film speaking "about" those women. But Trinh voiced a different approach in her voice-over; the film would be an exercise in "speaking nearby" (Chen, 1992). This means we pay attention to the location of the person and the text doing the speaking, both their geographic locations and their positions with respect to their living subjects (the people "in" the film) and the film's subject matters (what it addresses); in Trinh's words, this mode of speaking "reflects on itself and can come very close to a subject without, however, seizing or claiming it" (p. 87). To speak nearby is to attempt a kind of expressive proximity or even semantic allyship: a willingness to stand "with" those near whom one speaks while also trying to avoid a posture of objectivity.

Let me start by emphasizing the considerable distance that sits between Trinh's efforts at decolonizing documentary in the early 1980s and a reexamination of metadata conceptualizations in the early 2020s. It's important to keep this distance in mind, recognizing key differences in purpose, context and medium, among others. And yet that doesn't mean we ought not put them in conversation. Here the generative overlap is that crucial element of world languages: prepositions. These are short words (also called adpositions and not always words per se) that fly under the radar, all the while doing essential communicative work (Kurzon & Alder, 2008; Hagège, 2010). Speaking of English in particular—and not pretending that English can serve as a stand-in for all languages—the linguist R. M. W. Dixon says that prepositions "play a vital role in the language": they "indicate how and where, when and why, purpose and association, inclusion, connection, and many other things" (Dixon, 2022, p. vii).

Dixon's list is apt for considering prepositions as they bear upon the current discussion. Trinh saw in the use of "about" a mode of distanced description that maintains a veneer of neutrality. She then engaged in a practice of prepositional substitution, a practice that opened up other kinds of purposes, associations, inclusions and connections in filmmaking. Prepositional substitution in the case of metadata conceptualizations is both similar and different. What is similar is the questioning of "about" as the seemingly obvious and objective preposition to describe what metadata is, are and do. (It's worth noting that "data" and "metadata" are used as both singular or plural nouns; I tend to employ the singular for readability.) What is different is how we respond. We aren't necessarily looking for a different way of making and managing metadata per se, although that is certainly a path of inquiry that can be and has been followed, as with feminist and anticolonial archival practices in which the "archivist cares about and for and with subjects" (Caswell & Cifor, 2016, p. 36), or what Itza A. Carbajal (2021, p. 103) calls a "communal metadata praxis." Rather, we are looking for ways of addressing metadata in which aboutness is no longer the singular genetic element or the boundary line, when other versions and instantiations of metadata are analyzed and reworked. In short, we test prepositional substitution as a tool for remaking the landscape of metadata conceptualizations, and we do so with attention to the past, present and future of alternative worlds—those not defined by the hierarchies and pathologies of capitalism and colonialism.

Here a simple phrase comes to mind: "data near data." Whereas the preposition "about" is only sometimes spatial, tending to refer to situations and matters of concern, the preposition "near" is specifically spatial, carrying the basic meaning of "in the vicinity of." The term can also be "extended to cover physical and mental conditions," as in "Agatha was near despair all winter" (Dixon, 2022, p. 326). Applying that definition to metadata in an unfiltered way, we get phrases that echo Yanni Louikissas's mantra that "all data are local" (2019): data in the vicinity of data, information close to objects, a potentially informative statement alongside a potentially informative object, even data and information near people. To judge whether these are useful provocations is to judge whether they meaningfully answer this chapter's driving question with respect to what has been left out, overlooked or over-emphasized in conceptions of metadata.

Let's start by aligning several of the examples of metadata I have mentioned in this chapter:

(a) Social metadata. Across various platforms, there are fields for the display of metadata that depend on user contributions. These can be quantitative, such as like counts. They can also be qualitative, such as additions to the caption or description field.

(b) Hashtags. According to Elizabeth Losh, a hashtag is a type of metadata tag that "groups similarly tagged messages or allows an electronic search to return all messages that contain the same hashtag." Whether accompanied by a "word, abbreviation, acronym, or unspaced phrase," the hash character "tells the computer that a particular word or words should be read as more important than other words in a given message for purposes of sorting digital content into similar clusters" (Losh, 2020, p. 2).

(c) TK labels. As Montenegro (2019, p. 739) summarizes, TK (traditional knowledge) labels are "a set of 17 digital tags that can be included as associated metadata into diverse digital information contexts—CMSs, online catalogs and databases, finding aids, and online platforms—assisting in the recognition of, and education about, culturally appropriate circulation, access, and use of Indigenous cultural materials." As part of an "extra-legal initiative," these tags "draw from and extend already existing community protocols as their base," and they specifically diverge from universal standards, such as Dublin Core, that, as Montenegro shows, are incommensurate with many Indigenous understandings, uses and protocols for cultural materials.

Now, to look at these examples from the perspective of "data about data" is to see the throughlines that have tended to inform a great deal of metadata discourse: there are forms of secondary data; these data do different kinds of description; and that work of description supports storage, access and retrieval.

To look at these examples from the perspective of "data near data" and its correlates is quite different. For a start, we see that we are not in the territory of essences and either/ors. That's not to say the different examples are secretly all about vicinity. It's to say that there is the potential for multiple kinds of relations. Metadata might be a field of, as it were, prepositional and relational abundance.

Adopting this pluralistic way of looking, we get multiple versions of what nearness can mean in the context of metadata. Most basic (but not for that reason any less important) is a variable I'll call *visible position*. A significant number of metadata types and metadata examples derive part of their meaning and function from being nearby. That nearby location can be quite fixed. For instance, the variations on social metadata that attend posts are located where the app design beckons them to be placed. The location can be modestly variable. A user can decide where to place hashtags and in what order, whether within the body of a description or in a collection that follows a description. And the location can also be a matter of interruption. When TK labels are affixed to an entry in a database, they are there to interrupt an otherwise established view. They are there to be read and understood for different ways of understanding and interacting with that object. The TK labels assert a position that would not otherwise exist: a place for community protocols.

All of this could sound like a mistake of categories, as though we were talking about expression, interpretation and use when we should be talking about management and access. It is at this juncture that premises within the study of visual culture prove helpful. Losh says that

> critics of visual culture assume viewers are inculcated into seeing specific things, and they are also trained to block out things and render them invisible. In this way everything from an evidence photograph to a medical scan to a frame-grab of online video is seen through the lens of prior education that disciplines how eyes scan the visual field.
>
> (p. 53)

For Losh, hashtags are not somehow observers of or even just side players in these processes of visual discipline. Hashtags likewise "train the eye and set expectations about what to see" (p. 54). (She gives the example of materials tagged with #Love during the variously named 2014 Maidan Revolution in Ukraine. "The expectation for these images," writes Losh, "would be that they offer a vision of cooperation rather than conflict, such as shots of egalitarian interactions that convey the positive emotions associated with a leaderless revolution in which everyone participates.") Losh does not say that this dimension of hashtags is a dimension of nearness, but it is arguably implicit in the account. After all, these hashtags couldn't do this work—and TK labels couldn't do their interruptive pedagogy—without being near and readable. Not only that, these proximate metadata are indications of other kinds of mental and conceptual locations: positions and perspectives that the viewer/reader/user can see the content as addressed to or apparent places within hierarchies of interest, popularity or other dimensions of which the post is representative.

The latter notion suggests another variable at the intersection of metadata and nearness: what we might call *tactical approximation*. Consider this advice from *Popular Science* (any number of similar examples could have been selected): "If you need inspiration for finding related hashtags (or coming up with more to add to your own videos), try the Hashtag Generator for TikTok online, where you can type the name of a label and the platform will show you a list of similar ones you can use and tell you how popular they are" (Nield, 2022). Should people on TikTok follow these instructions, they will be exploring and considering (and having a database and algorithm tell them) what is in the relative referential orbit of their video and proposed hashtags. Some users might take the work of figuring out proximate hashtags as an interpretive or even expressive exercise, concluding, for instance, that #capitalism should sit alongside a video on climate, or that the issue of #extraction is worth asserting near a discussion of a recent report on museum commissioning practices. At the same time, as the advice I've quoted indicates, there is no purity of purpose in figuring out the strings of metadata that are potentially proximate to social media content. Metadata choices can easily be just a matter of present popularity: appending this hashtag to this content is an attempt at expanding the post's circulation, as with adding #cute to a post that is nothing of the sort. Aboutness is certainly in play here, but that term tends to privilege frames of truth and falsity. When we look at the full spectrum of meta elements, including those that are highly structured, those frames don't hold. Metadata producers often value the sufficiently close and the tactically proximate. That can be the case when content creators labor over their metadata, hoping to put their materials and handles into phones and eyeballs and minds. (Content creators are also metadata creators.) It can also be the case when catalogers engaged in reparative description revise the false and harmful categorizations and summaries of the past, replacing these false and harmful approximations with better, feasible and yet also imperfect approximations of just meta information in the present.

Of course, it isn't only people who produce, position and read metadata; these are also things done by various profit-driven technologies—machines, software and algorithms—and this gets us to a third version of metadata through the lens of nearness, what we can call *hidden vicinity*. The messaging app WhatsApp provides an especially helpful example. The straight story of the platform is that the messages you send are end-to-end encrypted, meaning they can't be read by the company; they can only be read by the people who have the encryption keys. And yet the metadata that accompanies and is produced by these exchanges is not encrypted. The company can track and share (does track and share) with whom you message, when and how, and these forms of metadata can coincide with or be integrated with other forms of computational metadata more difficult to trace and summarize, as Cooke (2020) lays out. Meredith Whitaker, the current president of Signal, a messaging app that does encrypt its metadata, explains: WhatsApp "collects the information about your profile, your profile photo, who is talking to whom, who is a group member. That is powerful metadata. It is particularly powerful—and this is where we have to back out into a structural argument—for a company to collect the data that is also owned by Meta/Facebook. Facebook has a huge amount, just unspeakable volumes, of intimate information about billions of people across the globe. It is not trivial to point out that WhatsApp metadata could easily be joined with Facebook data, and that it could easily reveal extremely intimate information about people" (Patel, 2022).

In a sense, I have already introduced the phenomenon this example suggests: I have spoken to the ways that social media posts serve as avenues for businesses to learn something about the user or the categories of people they're deemed to occupy (however unreliably, however cynically). What I have left out, however, are the dual dimensions of proximity and obscurity in all this. This is a complex terrain to navigate—that's part of the point—but the label "hidden vicinity" might sufficiently condense the dynamics taking place. For one thing, there is the sense in which the metadata extraction is not advertised or indicated as such, unlike the encryption of the content; it is hidden and even purposely obscured, as Cooke (2020) suggests. Then there is the fact that this metadata extraction is occurring right alongside the interaction; it is a feature lurking with and alongside the practice of speaking. Then, there is what coincides with the extraction, as Zuboff (2019) and many others have spoken to. The extraction from the obscured environment serves injections of material into the visible environment. The content you see, the suggestions you receive, the advertisements that appear, when and how these things occur—all of this is a matter of what can find its way near you, close enough that it can be received and acted on. In other words, the cycles of interaction—content, algorithm, data, metadata, analysis, delivery—are implicitly geared toward keeping one close, keeping one coming back and shaping a subject who is near their phone, near their devices, in the vicinity of a potential purchase or a potential vote. Proximity is power.

In stark contrast to hidden vicinity is one final variation on metadata and nearness I'll emphasize; it is a variation I suggest is embodied in TK labels. One thing they seem to say on aggregate harkens back to both Trinh's intervention and those of the artists who see in aboutness the striated, extractive ways of seeing and collecting that distinguish colonial modernity. TK labels suggest a way of conceiving and understanding metadata that is not centered in the speed and generality and consistency of knowing (and having the implicit, even "imperial right" to assert) what anything in the world is about (Azoulay, 2019), but that is instead centered in the caution, texture and relationality of knowing when and how to interact with what is, for the moment, near, or of knowing when something ought not, or ought not yet, be near. If the implicit paradigm of metadata has been access on demand for those in a position to act on that access, TK labels suggest a different paradigm, one that might be tentatively labeled *careful and contingent proximity*. Montenegro's reading of TK labels as a "form of contestation" is especially apt here. At one level, she shows the concrete ways these labels insist on careful and contingent relations and engagement. For example, the Seasonal label, used by the Pokagon Band of Potawatomi Indians, serves to "indicate that the circulating material should only be heard and/or utilized at a particular time of the year" (p. 740). As another example, the Secret/Sacred label has been used by the Sq'éwlets people to let "external users know that the material that is circulating should not be publicly available due to its secret, sacred, or esoteric components" (p. 741). At another level, Montenegro shows how the use of the labels exceeds any particular function. She says that the labels "broadly convey Indigenous concerns around access, circulation, and use," and that they eschew use as "a fixed application profile within a particular standard." Instead, they "work as a mechanism that refuses to erase the hegemonic condition of standard metadata fields, leaving those exclusionary terms visible and evident"—keeping these terms nearby—while also contributing to "the enactment of Indigenous peoples' inherent right to control and govern the gathering, management, circulation, access, use and interpretation of their own data, thus contributing to tribal self-determination, data governance and, ultimately, sovereignty" (p. 743).

This question of appearance, circulation and care implies another prepositional strand. In her account of hashtags through the lens of visual culture, Losh doesn't only emphasize the level of the individual person or image. She also points to the work of hashtags at the wider scales of aggregates of images, or even the broader and more diffuse phenomenon Jacques Rancière labels the "distribution of the sensible." "In many ways hashtags are a mechanism for the redistribution of the sensible," Losh (2020, p. 56) observes,

> by making particular kinds of content more perceptible to potential audiences. . . . The act of labeling a chunk of data shines a spotlight on it for a heterogeneous audience that may be composed of both activists seeking to reach a critical mass of participants and security forces planning their crackdown on a crowd of unruly dissidents.
>
> Losh (2020, p. 56)

In other words, the label or labels that are added to a given "chunk of data" are not just in an informative relationship with that chunk (about), nor are they also posited as somehow expressively or tactically proximate (near); they are also there in an active and supporting role, serving to facilitating that chunk's appearance or persistence in the spotlight, or, to speak near TK labels, those materials' considered and accepted passage in and out of circulation.

The preposition that comes to mind for these relational dynamics is "for"; these hashtags could be understood as acting "on behalf." Part of the facilitating work they do is to aid in the distribution (or non-distribution) of what is considered the central "content." Further work is for audiences. The hashtag "says" something informative about an event or an idea, but it supports the apparent informational needs of one who would care about this topic. Without it, the participants might not see the content in question; the metadata counters a potential scarcity or missed opportunity. Of course, as Losh emphasizes, hashtags can also work on behalf of security forces looking to quell dissent, or they can serve as reservoirs of data about people for the larger machines of attention and engagement. And none of this is restricted to hashtags: many contributions to social metadata carry with them metadata elements for which the operations "for" are active and real, even if harder to precisely quantify or summarize. The difficulty of naming and analyzing certain meta relations doesn't make them any less significant.

From "about" to "near" to "for"—as I hope is obvious, much more could be said about the two additions, and the list of prepositions can easily grow. (For instance, hashtags suggest metadata can exist "with" or even "in" other data and information, and we also need to consider relations like "against" and "from.") But the more pressing concern for present purposes is whether the provocation "data near data" has meaningfully altered our conceptual purchase on metadata.

I contend that it has. Not only have we managed to evade what we might hazard calling the "hegemony of aboutness," but we have also been able to see one further reason that metadata is not just data about data. Whether as individual items, aggregates, or even taxonomies and ontologies, metadata bears more varied and complex prepositional relations than the normative frame of aboutness lets on. My contention is that those prepositional relations exist and matter. My further contention is that the slogan data about data occludes rather than illuminates them. The critiques of the phrase get us some way there, but it is necessary to go further—to dispense with the non-natural and non-neutral assumption that it's all about aboutness. Metadata is far more abundant in social and expressive relations than both the default and corrective definitions would indicate, and "data near data" is an effective, if necessarily imperfect, initial corrective, one that seeks to place decolonial, anticapitalist and other intersecting critical perspectives at the heart of the discussion.

Metadata Beyond Aboutness

Many questions remain, such as how different meta and prepositional relations interact, the need for more cultural and linguistic specificity with respect to both literal prepositions and adpositions and their analogues in metadata, or whether and how to extend the concept of metadata to pre-computational and non-machine-readable creations (Weinberger, 2007). Rather than address such questions all too quickly, I'll close by returning to those that have driven this chapter. What might be done differently in inquiry and practice when prepositional abundance is a given? And how should the landscape of metadata conceptualization be altered to accommodate the perspectives I've explored here?

Taking a cue from metadata's fluidity and ambivalence, I'll answer not just one way but several. One possibility is that we could basically slightly append the standing approach to say that metadata is effectively data about* data or a potentially informative statement about* a potentially informative object, with the asterisks indicating the inevitable presence of other prepositional modes. The appeal of this approach is its mix of simplicity and open-endedness; the asterisk can hold space for any number of reasons why aboutness should be qualified, from Pomerantz's emphasis on subjectivity to much more involved and indeed politically informed critiques, including those that frame aboutness as a fundamentally colonial construct. And yet, it seems that these affordances come at a cost. For one thing, the use of about* leaves the frame of aboutness firmly intact, a status that is open to objection along not just the lines of precision but also of value and power. The use of the asterisk also risks confining interpretation and expression to the margins of debate, allowing the discussion to revolve around managing objects and information, when the kinds of examples I've assembled here suggest the vibrancy in expressive meta statements and performative data utterances, and when scores of people regularly engage with metadata in exactly these terms. Finally, the use of the asterisk doesn't get at the dynamics of power I identified earlier. It does nothing to indicate the non-neutrality of the concept, nor the role metadata might play in repair, nor the potential for new conceptions (or refusals) of the phenomenon from decolonial, anticolonial and antiracist positions.

A more thorough embrace of the implications of prepositional substitution leads us to more intensive proposals. One option is to build on Koster and Kreil's provocation that we ought to effectively stop using the term metadata. We could say that metadata in the context of social media and widespread surveillance reveals all the trouble with the term metadata: that hashtags can count, with all their varieties of functions, would seem to reveal how confusing and superfluous the original concept always was, and how it's much better to recognize everything out there as data. Taking this position further, we would get to the idea that there are many types of data and information in the world, and that hashtags and other things we call metadata are better understood now as pieces and sets of information with multiple prepositional functions and switches built into them. To that end, we could coin a term that would subtly but meaningfully distinguish particular types of data produced by people and machines: "prepositional data." These would be data that serve to indicate and mediate "how and where, when and why, purpose and association, inclusion, connection, and many other things." I can imagine further study of both individual prepositions and their interrelationships. I can also imagine analysis of how prepositional data can shed that distinguishing prepositional feature, coming to be treated as "just data," with this switch of status often taking place in the shadows.

Another option—the last I'll indicate—is to move away from the focus on definitions. After all, there is another equally significant dimension to the landscape of metadata conceptualizations. Mayernik (2020) speaks to it:

> If the notion of 'metadata' has been defined in a variety of ways, it has been categorized and conceptualized in an even more diverse fashion.

Categorizations of metadata reflect the different conceptions and motivations of the people who generate them, and manifest in a variety of metadata typologies.

Mayernik gives many examples of these categorizations, such as the "constructed, constructive, actionable" triad, or the five types laid out by Gilliland (2008): administrative, descriptive, preservation, use and technical. This second set is especially relevant to the questions I've raised here; it is the kind of typology that tends to accompany "data about data," whether this is in lectures, textbooks, explanatory videos or the results of web searches. The typology acts as an entrance point and initial filter for many people first introduced to metadata; it also structures projects and even professions.

From the perspective of this chapter, an intervention at the level of categories suggests additions rather than deletions. Several are already on the table. When institutional actors engage in the work of altering or newly developing metadata toward antiracist and anticolonial ends, they can be said to be in the practice of thinking, producing and enacting *reparative metadata*, and that category suggests other crucial kinds, such as *decolonial* and *anticolonial metadata*. A further addition was implicit in my discussion of nearness. As we have seen, hashtags can certainly function in the mode of descriptive metadata, but quite often they function in a mode that is closer to speech. They serve as statements in themselves, or the statements they make in themselves come into dialogue with the notions, feelings or ideas in what is otherwise considered the primary material. This is a version of metadata we can dub *expressive metadata*. Here "expressive" refers to the work of mediating—conveying, showing, assembling—thoughts, feelings and ideas. A further addition was implicit in the discussion of "forness": *distributive metadata*. These would be metadata that help distribute pieces of content through informational networks; they support that content's spread, though they can also be as much "about" circulating themselves as they are about circulating given content. As much is evident in political hashtags that assert a norm or a value, but it is also the case with other hashtags. These become complex entities in themselves, entities that manage to maintain or expand their distribution through their yoking to other materials and other metadata.

If there is a potential downside to these additions to the core typology of metadata, it is that they do not necessarily answer all the lines of critique of data about data. For example, the concerns of Pomerantz and Kreil persist: the seeming need to maintain the frame of information, or the concern that, at this point in the game, it's all just data and mostly data about people. One potential answer to these doubts is to take the inclusion of "expressive" metadata seriously. We can see in the rise of expressive metadata the implication that the world of metadata—its name notwithstanding—isn't strictly a world of data. We might even venture to think of metadata as a cultural form for which data and information have historically been the dominant frames and modes but for which other frames and modes are possible, including the layers of expression, the positing of relationships, and metadata as a "compilation of words used to express ideas, feelings, emotions, and values" (Carbajal, 2021, p. 102). Some of the most powerful uses of social metadata—the kinds that have helped spark protests, change minds and move policies—have been those that take up this meaning-attentive approach. They creatively combine metadata types: the reparative with the descriptive, the distributive with the expressive. At the same time, as many of the writers I have cited in these pages would emphasize, it remains to be seen whether these critical and inter-sectional uses of metadata can overcome and outlast that most persistent of metadata types: the extractive.

References

Adler, M. (2016). The case for taxonomic reparations. *Knowledge Organization, 43*(8), 630–640.

Ashbel, A. E. (2019, August). An argument against aboutness. *Vorherbst Magazine.* www.steirischerherbst.at/de/vorherbst/591/an-argument-against-aboutness.

Azoulay, A. A. (2019). *Potential history: Unlearning imperialism.* Verso.

Bagley, P. R. (1968). *Extension of programming language concepts.* University City Science Center.

Berwald, O. (2016, Spring). Against aboutness: The corpse that almost got away. *The Scofield, 1*(4), 196–197.

Carbajal, I. A. (2021). Historical metadata debt: Confronting colonial and racist legacies through a post-custodial metadata praxis. *Across the Disciplines, 18*(1–2), 91–107.

Caswell, M., & Cifor, M. (2016). From human rights to feminist ethics: Radical empathy in the archives. *Archivaria,* 23–43.

Chen, N. N. (1992). 'Speaking nearby': A conversation with Trinh T. Minh-ha. *Visual Anthropology Review, 8*(1), 82–91.

Commission on Federal Paperwork. (1977). *Reference manual for program and information officials: A handbook for managers* (Vol. 1 of a 2). Part Manual. Commission on Federal Paperwork.

Cooke, T. N. (2020). Metadata, jailbreaking, and the cybernetic governmentality of iOS: Or, the need to distinguish digital privacy from digital privacy. *Surveillance & Society, 18*(1), 90–103.

Dixon, R. M. W. (2022). *English prepositions: Their meanings and uses.* Oxford University Press.

Exposing the Invisible. (2016, May 11). *Michael Kreil: An honest picture of metadata.* https://exposingtheinvisible.org/en/articles/michael-kreil

Frick, R. L., & Proffitt, M. (2022). *Reimagine descriptive workflows: A community-informed agenda for reparative and inclusive descriptive practice.* OCLC Research.

Furner, J. (2020). Definitions of 'metadata': A brief survey of international standards. *Journal of the Association for Information Science and Technology, 71*(6), E33–E42.

Gilliland, A. J. (2008). Setting the stage. In *Introduction to metadata: Pathways to digital information* (3rd ed.). M. Baca. Getty Information Institute.

Hagège, C. (2010). *Adpositions*. Oxford University Press.

Holley, R. M., & Joudrey, D. N. (2021). Aboutness and conceptual analysis: A review. *Cataloging & Classification Quarterly, 59*(2–3), 159–185.

Koster, L. (2015, June 16). *Standard deviations in data modeling, mapping and manipulation*. https://commonplace.net/2015/06/standard-deviations

Kurzon, D., & Adler, S. (2008). *Adpositions: Pragmatic, semantic and syntactic perspectives*. John Benjamins Publishing Company.

Losh, E. (2020). *Hashtag*. Bloomsbury Academic.

Loukissas, Y. A. (2019). *All data are local: Thinking critically in a data-driven society*. MIT Press.

Mayernik, M. S. (2020). Metadata. *Knowledge Organization, 47*(8), 696–713.

Méndez, E., & van Hooland, S. (2014). Metadata typology and metadata uses. In M.-A. Sicilia (Ed.), *Handbook of metadata, semantics and ontologies* (pp. 9–39). World Scientific.

Montenegro, M. (2019). Subverting the universality of metadata standards: The TK labels as a tool to promote indigenous data sovereignty. *Journal of Documentation, 75*(4), 731–749.

Nield, D. (2022, August 15). 7 Tricks to make the most of TikTok. *Popular Science*. www.popsci.com/diy/tiktok-tips

Parry, K. (2023). *A theory of assembly: From museums to memes*. University of Minnesota Press.

Patel, N. (2022). Why signal won't compromise on encryption, with president Meredith Whittaker. *The Verge*. www.theverge.com/23409716/signal-encryption-messaging-sms-meredith-whittaker-imessage-whatsapp-china

Pomerantz, J. (2015). *Metadata*. MIT Press.

Raina, K., & Smith, J. (2018). Q&A with Alice Tippit. *Maake Magazine*. www.maakemagazine.com/alice-tippit

Ranger, J. (2012, September 19). *9 reasons you understand more about media preservation than you think*. https://blog.weareavp.com/9-reasons-you-understand-more-about-media-preservation-than-you-think

Smith, L. T. (2021). *Decolonizing methodologies: Research and indigenous peoples* (3rd ed.). Zed Books.

Weinberger, D. (2007). *Everything is miscellaneous: The power of the new digital disorder*. Henry Holt and Company.

Wenner, S. (2021). Aesthetics of Mykorrhiza. The practice of *apparatus*. In C. Stalpaert et al. (Eds.), *Performance and posthumanism: Staging prototypes of composite bodies* (pp. 93–109). Springer.

Yablo, S. (2014). *Aboutness*. Princeton University Press.

Zuboff, S. (2019). *The age of surveillance capitalism: The fight for a human future at the new frontier of power*. Public Affairs.

3 Social Media Use in the Sudanese Uprising, 2018

Mediating Civilian-Military Discourse

Mustafa Taha

Introduction

The Internet and especially social media have been hailed as the principal elements in expanding political participation by reducing the cost of access to alternative sources of information (Garrett, 2006; Howard, 2011) and facilitating coordination (Castells, 2012; Earl & Kimport, 2011). Mass media outlets are highly regulated and controlled in authoritarian societies and act as mouthpieces of governments. In such situations, alternative information can only be obtained by having access to online sources, including social media (Reuter & Szakonyi, 2015). Scholars have argued that alternative sources of information are vital for raising political awareness and expressing social discontent (Hollyer et al., 2015; Tang &Huhe, 2014; Coffé, 2017). Social media proved to be indispensable tools for activists to gain vital information and make informed political judgments (McDonald & Thompson, 2016; Keck & Sikkink, 2014; Couldry et al., 2016). Kirkizh and Koltsova (2021) found that "the effect of online news consumption is strongest in autocracies and weakest in transitional regimes" (p. 8). Valenzuela et al. (2012) found a positive correlation between online news consumption, particularly Facebook news, and protest participation.

Increased political awareness and knowledge of competing policy options can boost political engagement, including protest activities (Meirowitz & Tucker, 2013; Keck & Sikkink, 2014; Wukich, 2016). Combined with other contributing factors, this process can lead to political upheavals or even the downfall of entire regimes (Hollyer et al., 2015). Howard (2011) suggests that exposing hidden political, social and economic news online can raise general discontent among the public. Kirkizh and Koltsova (2021) concur with Hollyer et al. (2015) and argue that the availability of economic information in non-democratic societies could destabilize both transitional and consolidated autocratic regimes.

Extant research dealt with questions pertaining to the efficacy of social media in helping activist to communicate, organize and mobilize in protests (Loader et al., 2016; Eltantawy & Wiest, 2011). Nonetheless, social media

DOI: 10.4324/9781003299912-3

architecture and ownership are centralized leaving little space for activists to "reprogram their communication spaces" (Lovink, 2019, p. 27).

Some studies addressed social media shortcomings and have demonstrated a positive relationship between online alternative media use and protest (Leung & Lee, 2014) as well as explicating some of the mechanisms in which different uses of social network sites can influence protest participation (Valenzuela, 2013; Brundidge et al., 2014; Ladd & Lenz, 2009; Vissers et al., 2012; Wojcieszak et al., 2016). According to Dutta and Bhat (2016), Twitter users are more interested and engaged in politics compared to users of traditional media.

Chan (2017) examined the role of social media in social protests with an emphasis on identity, efficacy and anger, and demonstrated the benefits of interdisciplinary theoretical integration to better understand news media use in collective action. Political communication alone cannot be a primary driver of social unrest. Social media use should be understood as a nexus among other structural factors including "corruption, hardship, and repression" (Norris, 2012, p. 5). To have a better understanding of what had happened during the Arab Spring, Comunello and Anzera (2012) advised Internet researchers have some knowledge of international relations theory. Relying on a context-based approach, Bellin (2012) examined social media use in addition to long-standing grievances, an emotional trigger, and a sense of impunity as explanatory factors that triggered social unrest in Tunisia and Egypt. According to Karatzogianni (2015), emphasizing social media as primary factor for the Arab Spring protests ignores important contextual elements, reduces social actors in these countries to "homogeneous groups" equally manipulated by ICTs. In the same vein, Wolfsfeld et al. (2013) recommend scholars consider political context when examining the relationship between social media use and political protests. Keating and Melis (2017a) studied young adults' use of social media and argue that social media is not re-engaging those who have already lost interest in politics.

A number of studies have discussed social media effects on political participation (Kirkizh & Koltsova, 2021; Theocharis & Lowe, 2016) as well as their effects on protests (Enikolopov et al., 2020; Tufekci & Wilson, 2012). Both Oser et al. (2013) and Schlozman et al. (2012, p. 515) found a causal relationship between online political engagement and young adults' education and socio-economic status (SES) and suggested that online political engagement resonates with the inequalities in offline participation. Feezell's (2016, p. 502) cites income as the only predictor of access to the Internet rather than online political engagement. On the other hand, Keating and Melis (2017b) describes political interest as a driving force in online political engagement among young adults, rather than their educational or socio-economic resources. Several scholars have referred to an association between online political expression and offline political engagement (Theocharis & Quintelier, 2014; Yamamoto et al., 2013). Avril and Melis (2017) concluded that although social media may provide new opportunities, "it is not re-engaging the young adults who have already lost interest in politics" (p. 877).

As profitable business models, social media platforms are replete with advertising and marketing information. They capitalize on algorithmic manipulations of the newsfeeds, information curation and the filter bubble effect in apps to send persuasive, personalized advertising messages (Lovink, 2019, p. 27). The notion suggesting that the Internet and social media represent equalizers leveling the field for disadvantaged groups is challenged. Corporate and influential political elites continue to dominate online conversations, reproducing offline inequalities in cyberspace (Curran et al., 2012, pp. 13–14).

A considerable body of research studied the "Arab Spring" and demonstrated that protestors used social media to coordinate actions and report upon the events (Rane & Salem, 2012; Gerbaudo, 2012; Castells, 2012). The Tunisian uprising has been part of a wave of protest movements spanning the Arab world, termed the *Arab Spring*. These movements have given rise to a multitude of questions that have looked at the social, economic and political factors that came together to bring about the Arab Spring. It is argued that social media played a crucial role in the uprising (Breuer, 2016).

Since the unfolding of the Arab uprisings in the Middle East in 2011, scholarly interest has focused on the role of social media in general and Facebook and Twitter in particular. Researchers reflected on how Egyptian protestors setup Facebook groups, such as "We are all Khaled Said," and used Twitter hashtags, such as #egypt to exchange messages (Lim, 2012; Lotan et al., 2011; Musa, 2014).

The notion of empowerment was highlighted giving social media as new communication technologies a prime role in the uprising. By foregrounding the role of social media, the role of the protesters who paid in blood and tears to bring about political change is unwittingly downplayed. Social media was instrumental in the political change but was not the decisive factor in bringing about the social change that ensued. In recent years, the unsurmountable economic hardships and fluid nature of political strife have illustrated that social media can be creatively used within a nexus of other contextual factors to aid sociopolitical movements (Cottle, 2011).

The Sudanese uprising of 2018 succeeded in removing Gen. Bashir as a president at a hefty economic, social and political cost. During his pro-Islamist rule, Sudan was an authoritarian police state, where mass media were tightly controlled and political dissent often was punished or crushed. The advent of the Internet and new information and communication technologies, including social media, enabled young Sudanese to communicate, organize and protest in creative ways, bypassing the control of the state.

This chapter will use the narratives of Sudanese young men and women who participated in the 2019 uprising to explore four research questions. First, how did the protesters use social media to raise awareness, mobilize and coordinate protests during the uprising of 2018? Second, how did the protesters use social media to disseminate oppositional narratives challenging the government's narratives? Third, how did the government respond to the protesters' activities? Finally, why did the government resort to Internet blackout during the dispersal of the sit-in? Answering these questions gives important insights on the complex ways in which social movements utilize social media to challenge a repressive regime. The study does not attempt to quantify the Sudanese protesters use of social media or to glamourize their reliance on it to achieve the goals of the uprising. The study aspires to shed light on the various facets of interactions that occurred on social media during the uprising.

The December 2018 Uprising

Social movements represent complex political phenomena arising from an interplay of economic, social and political factors. In the Sudanese scenario, these factors contributed substantially to the rise and development of the Sudanese political parties. The history of the modern Sudanese state started on January 1, 1956, when Sudan became an independent state after years of British colonial rule. The history of the modern Sudanese state followed a predictable trajectory. A civilian rule, followed by a military dictatorship that would be toppled by a popular uprising. A civilian government that declared independence in 1956, was replaced by Gen. Aboud's military rule in 1958. A popular uprising in October 1964 called for freedom and peace, toppled the military regime. A transitional government took over and prepared the country for parliamentary elections. The democratic government that ruled the country from 1964 to 1969 was overthrown by a military coup led by Colonel Jafar Nimeiry on May 25, 1969. The military government that espoused socialism and pan-Arabism failed to find a sustainable peace to the war in Southern Sudan and improve the lives of the Sudanese people. Economic hardship and imposition of the Sharia laws led to an escalation of the conflict in Southern Sudan and deterioration of the security situation in the country. A popular uprising led by trade unions succeeded in toppling Nimeiry's regime and instating a transitional civilian-led government on April 6, 1985. A civilian government led by Prime Minister Sadiq al-Mahdi failed to the stop the war in Southern Sudan and improve the lives of the Sudanese people. Sectarian bickering and political intrigues enabled political parties including the Muslim Brothers to infiltrate the military establishment to protect their interests.

On June 30, 1989, Gen. Omer al-Bashir assumed power in a military coup. The military takeover was considered by many as the brainchild of Hassan al-Turabi, the spiritual leader of the Muslim Brotherhood in Sudan. The government espoused Islamic laws, mobilized the youth for a jihadist war against the Southern Sudanese and endorsed a free-market economy. The Islamists purged the military and civil service of non-Islamists elements and recruited loyal Islamists in a policy known as empowerment (*Tamkeen*). Politically motivated economic privatization and direct foreign investment by Islamic banks led to unemployment and deterioration in the standard of living. Political pressure and economic sanctions imposed by Western countries, namely the United States forced the authoritarian rule of Gen. Bashir to accept the Comprehensive Peace Agreement (CPA) in 2005, a referendum on self-determination, and eventually the secession of Southern Sudan in 2011. The move was hailed by the Islamists and their supporters of as an important step to consolidate their power and sustain the so-called Islamic rule. The government used repressive measures to muzzle political dissent and engaged in a brutal war in the Western region of Darfur. As the security situation deteriorated, the government used more coercive measures to quell political unrest. Political maneuvering, carrot and stick, and divide and rule tactics helped Gen. Bashir weaken his political opponents and remain in power for almost 30 years. The popular uprising of April 6, 2019, resulted in the removal of Gen. Bashir from the political scene and the establishment of civilian-military rule on April 11, 2019.

During the December 2018 uprising, the protesters directed their action against the state's egregious infringement on the freedom, safety of innocent people in war zones and justice. These were the slogans that the Sudanese people raised during the uprising. The government tried to shirk its responsibility by framing the structural problems it created as individual failures and blamed the Sudanese people for pervasive ethnic conflicts, sectarian discord and lack of security. Young Sudanese protesters utilized social media to voice their disaffection and articulate their political preferences outside of the historical confines political engagement (Albaih, 2015). They formed groups and exchanged anti-government information on Facebook. On Twitter, they used descriptive hashtags to show their solidarity when a violent act occurred and tailored hashtags when they called for participation in the protests (UNDP, 2019).

Social media outlets provided unprecedented social spaces for activists to counter the government's narratives and vent their frustration with the power abuse, corruption and violations of human rights. They learned numerous lessons from the use of social media by protesters during the Arab Spring, the Occupy movement and other parts of southern Europe (Theocharis et al., 2015). In a number of countries, autocratic governments managed to control traditional media outlets, but they failed to control the Internet as an alternative source of information (Lorentzen, 2014). In Arab countries, new information and communication technologies pose a threat to hegemonic power structures that helped shape public opinion in the past (Miladi, 2016).

The dire economic situation was a leading factor galvanizing the Sudanese people to rise against Gen. Bashir authoritarian rule. Nonetheless, popular aspirations for dignity, both at the personal and communal level, were a critical lynchpin during the uprising. Removing a dictatorial rule and reclaiming human dignity was one of the aspirations of the protesters. Since the time of the Condominium Rule, the Sudanese people have overcome decades of exploitation, subjugation and protracted internal conflicts. Political and social strife arising from an identity crisis characterized post-independence Sudanese history. Western pressures and influence of petro-dollar money of Arab states encouraged the Sudanese ruling elites to espouse Arab nationalism during the 1970s and Muslim Brotherhood in the 1990s.

Role of Social Media in Protests: Communication, Mobilization, and Coordination

The concept of the public sphere is a useful theoretical framework for understanding the interplay between the protesters' use of social media and the government's response to their activities. A brief historical context can illustrate the presence of these themes, namely protesters' use of social media to topple the government and the latter's use of the state apparatus to quell the protests.

This study seeks to contribute to this literature by looking beyond the high-profile social protests to examine the extent to which young Sudanese adults used social media for political engagement including exchanging ideas and organizing demonstrations. Although young adults' social media use in political engagement has attracted academic interest (Kim & Amna, 2015; Xenos et al., 2014), little attention is given to exploratory studies examining social media and political protest in east and central African countries.

Habermas et al. (1974) defined public sphere as an arena of social life containing various formations of public opinions. Habermas discussed the influence alternative publics could have on the public sphere and acknowledged their resistance to mass-mediated re-presentations of society and their ability to create their own political interventions. Having in mind monetary influences that contradict the essence of public sphere, Habermas (1989, 1991) questioned the potency of these alternative public spheres and their influence in the political sphere. Habermas (2006, p. 415) highlights "reciprocity between speakers and addressees" and argues that new media is incapable of revitalizing the public sphere. Kruse et al. (2018) challenge Habermas' notion of the public sphere on social media and argued that younger generations avoid communicative action resulting from online political discourse out of fear and surveillance.

Downey and Fenton (2003) argued that the "mass-media public sphere will become more open to radical opinion as a result of the coincidence of societal crises and the growth of virtual counter-public spheres" (p. 199). The influence of Sufi Islam requires a critical look at the concept of the public sphere in the Sudanese context. The emergence of the Sudanese diaspora and Western notions of freedom and democracy as counter-public spheres created considerable influence on political discourse in the Sudanese Sufi dominated public sphere. Although the impact did not translate directly into a dramatic social change, social media provided new opportunities and spaces within which political contests are manifested (Lim, 2012, p. 234).

Thus, the Sudanese public sphere can be envisioned as a space within which multiple interpretations of political and social issues are projected. Nonetheless, the government's narrative continues to have a dominant voice in that public sphere.

Social Media and Political Protest in North Africa

Hall's encoding/decoding model (1991, 2003), particularly the notion of oppositional reading of media messages, and Fuchs' (2010) conceptualization of social media as critical media are useful theoretical underpinnings for understanding social media use in the Sudan. Government control over media organizations and its hegemonic ideology incorporated by message encoders are met with oppositional reading by opponents revealing a degree of resistance to the content of media texts (Woodstock, 2016). The voices of protesters and marginalized people who have been traditionally under represented or excluded by the government in the public sphere, found an alternative place vent their grievances and criticize governmental policies on social media (Fuchs, 2010). Online political activism in other parts of the world, particularly neighboring Egypt (Lim, 2012), could have inspired the Sudanese political activists.

Protest movements have known that authoritarian governments could use all available means to undermine protesters' efforts on the ground and on social media. Physical control over the infrastructure of information and communication technologies enabled authoritarian governments to retaliate against protesters in various stages of mobilizations (Howard & Hussain, 2013).

Examples in the Middle East, namely in Tunisia and Egypt, suggest that governments used coercion and brutality to suppress online activists (Younis, 2007; Faris, 2013). Couldry (2013) indicates that corporate social media entities that profit from consumer-generated content on their platforms may simultaneously serve the interests of the state. Lorentzen (2014) contends that authoritarian governments may not be capable of controlling alternative sources of information, such as the Internet. Bodrunova and Litvinenko (2013) refer to a strong association between protest participation and news consumption in fragile democracies where governments cannot effectively control social media and the Internet. Some scholars argue that consolidated autocracies may control all media markets including online outlets (Coffé, 2017).

Tufekci and Wilson (2012) found that those who participated from the first day of the demonstrations in the Egyptian uprising had used Facebook more proactively compared to those who joined the protests later. Brym et al. (2014) found that demonstrators, during the 2011 Egyptian uprising, used short messages (SMS) and had more trust in new media. Herrera (2014) has shown how social media can work as a liberating force but also as a site of struggle between rival forces, the United States, the Muslim Brotherhood and the Egyptian military, who vie for control over the hearts and minds of the young. Some scholars challenged the potency of social media and concluded that the Egyptian revolution depended more on satellite and word-of-mouth than the contribution of social media (Wilson & Dunn, 2011; Lynch et al., 2017).

Howard (2011) indicated that the popularization of digital media would bring about social change and democratization of politics and cultures in Muslim countries. In the wake of the Egyptian revolution, Lynch et al. (2017) found that one role of social media is clustering, reinforcing in-group solidarity and out-group demonization. Howard and Hussain (2013) highlight the impact of ICT in empowering civil societies and underscore the crucial role of these societies in the Arab Spring. On the other hand, Hassanpour (2014) refers to the government-enforced media shutdown during the Egyptian uprising and shows significant correlations between protest dispersion and media disruption. He found that social media did not necessarily play a significant role in mobilization and coordinating the public protests.

The Sudanese Mediascape

Print

The government used strict regulatory policies, censorship and surveillance by its National Intelligence and Security Service (NISS) to control the press and crackdown on freedom of expression. Infamous repressive measures included confiscating copies, closing down offices and depriving newspapers from government and corporate advertising money.

Based on the 2017 newspaper circulation report (Eltigani, n.a.), there were 45 newspapers (29 political newspapers, 10 sports newspapers and 6 entertainment newspapers). All newspapers have online digital versions. The government continues to control the market, and pro-government newspapers record the highest levels of distribution. Influential newspapers included *Al-Ayaam*, *Al-Sudani*, *Al-Tayar*, *Al-Intibaha* and *Al-Maidan*, mouthpieces of the Sudanese Communist Party. *Alintibaha*, a pro-government newspaper, enjoyed a high level of distribution (19, 000 copies) due to governmental subscriptions.

Broadcast Media

Bashir's government, a one-party pro-Islamist state, maintained tight control over media organization and muzzled political opposition. It used various laws and regulations as well as the National Intelligence Security Service (NISS) to ensure total political control. The government bestowed economic support to the National Television and Radio Corporation (NTRC), the Sudanese News Agency (SUNA) and extended financial and technical assistance to local radio and television stations in the country.

There were more than 18 government-supported radio stations. They used FM frequencies and focused on education and entertainment. Stations popular for music and entertainment programs included *Mango 96 FM* and *Khartoum FM*. *Radio Dabanga*, Netherlands-based Internet radio, and *Afia Darfur*, Chad-based, were found to provide more representation for the people of Darfur (Eltigani, n.a.). Popular television channels included *Sudan TV*, *Al-Shurooq*, *Blue Nile*, *Sudaniya 24* and *Angham Music TV*. Having in mind that these channels act as mouthpieces for their financiers, the government tried to utilize satellite television to propagate its "Islamic Scheme" (Galander, 2020).

The advent of satellite television from Middle East countries attracted the attention of the Sudanese public, particularly entertainment content. Satellite television laid the groundwork for protesters and marginalized groups to voice their concerns and challenge the state's dominance in the public sphere. The influence of the Egyptian channels, as well as MBC (a Saudi-backed channel) and pro-Islamist Al Jazeera (Qatari-funded channel) news, talk shows and debates on satellite television in the region laid the groundwork for social media activism in the country. Al Jazeera beefed up its popularity by presenting itself as an embodiment of Islamic and Arab identity and a challenger to the hegemonic Western powers (Lynch, 2003).

Internet and Social Media

The government has control over the connectivity and can block all of the Internet gateways in the country when the National Intelligence Security Service (NISS) wants to slow down or block access to the Internet. In the past the Internet services witnessed frequent interruptions for technical as well as political reasons. The National Telecommunications Corporation (NTC) is in charge of regulating telecommunication activities in the country. The main telecommunications operations are MTN, Sudani and Zain, a Kuwaiti company. Zain increased its total number of customers to 12.5 million compared to Sudani (about 11 million subscribers) and MTN (about 7 million subscribers).

Social media platforms were extensively used by the Sudanese protesters between December 2018 and June 30, 2019, namely Facebook, YouTube, WhatsApp and Twitter. According to the Internet World Site, in 2017, out of 41.5 million Sudanese, only 28.6% accessed the Internet. Between January and December 2019, approximately 45% of social media usage in Sudan occurred on Facebook, 44% used YouTube and 6% used Twitter (Statcounter, 2019). WhatsApp is the most popular platform not just for news consumption but for socializing and entertainment. Sudanese youth and women groups on Facebook and WhatsApp became sites for discussion of various topics from self-grooming to organizing civil resistance (Ali, 2019, p. 122). Gossip, rumors and scandals publicized on the Sudanese social media sites sometimes received coverage in traditional media (Hofheinz, 2017, p. 283).

Social Media and Unfolding Political Developments

The secession of South Sudan, 2011, deprived the Sudanese government of an important source of oil revenue. The uprising of 2013 was in response rising cost of living and removal subsidies to basic consumer goods namely fuel. The government responded to widespread protests with a brutal crackdown that resulted in 200 deaths (Copnall, 2013). Due to minimal Internet penetration in Sudan, social media did not play a major role in the uprising (Hale, 2014; Hofheinz, 2017).

Protests that broke out in Damzeen and Atbara in 2018 in response to the rising cost of bread and fuel metamorphosed into calls for regime change. The Sudanese Professional Association (SPA), a loose umbrella of professionals' trade unions, emerged as an uncontested representative of protesters and assumed a leading role following the eruption of early demonstrations (Amin, 2019). The SPA called for demonstrations on April 4 and 6, 2019 using hashtags that included *#Mudun_al-Sudan_Tantafid* (Sudan's Cities Rise Up), *Mawakib al-Xubz wa al-Karama* (Protests of Bread and Dignity) and *Mawakib al-Sudan: al-Watan al-Wahid* (Protests of Sudan: One Nation) (Abushouk, 2021).

The SPA played an important role in unifying opposition groups and signing the Declaration of Freedom and Change on January 1, 2019 (Berridge, 2019). The Declaration called for dismantling Bashir's government and forming a technocratic transitional government in order to prepare the country for democratic elections. Four months of widespread protests, a sit-in in front of General Headquarters of Armed Forces and political wrangling among senior military officers resulted in removal of Bashir on April 11, 2019 (Patrick, 2019). A Transitional Military Council (TMC) led by Gen. Ibn Auf, an army was rejected by the protestors who claimed that the demand for a civilian rule had not been met (Burke, 2019). On April 12, 2019, Ibn Auf was forced to step down, allowing Gen. Abdelfattah al-Burhan to emerge as the de facto military head of state. Negotiations between the TMC and the Forces of Freedom and Change (FFC) started to form a transitional government to prepare the country for democratic elections. To exert pressure on the military, the SPA called on protesters to maintain the sit-in until the demands of the FFC were met (BBC News, 2019).

On June 3, 2019, military units primarily from the Rapid Support Forces (RSF) stormed the sit-in and opened fire on the protesters using a scorched-earth tactic (Malik, 2019). Reports emerging from the sit-in site documented incidents of rape, beatings and disposal of bodies in the River Nile. Activists and human rights groups suggest that more than 112 people were killed, and it is suspected that a number of corpses were disposed of in the river (Middle East Eye, 2019). Following that horrendous massacre, the government enforced a month-long Internet blackout (Bendimerad & Faisal, 2019; Yousef & Nafisa, 2019; Middle East Eye, 2019).

Sudanese activists and their allies in the diaspora used Twitter to grab international attention and gain support and sympathy for the peaceful Sudanese uprising in the wake of June 3, 2019. Popular hashtags included *#BlueforSudan*, *#SudanUprising* and *#IAmTheSudanRevolution*. The activists managed effective awareness campaigns, ensuring optimum frequency and wide reach through "trending" algorithms. One of the most popular hashtags, *#BlueforSudan*, highlighted the killing of Mohamed Hashim Mattar at the capital's sit-in site on June 3, 2019. The *#BlueforSudan* campaign asked social media users to turn their profile images into blue, Mattar's favorite color (Elmileik & Khalil, 2019).

A number of news articles highlighting the events in June 2019 were published on the hashtag in regional as well as international media (Elmileik & Khalil, 2019; Patrick, 2019). A number of activists in the diaspora (e.g., @ehabthebeast) made posts and uploaded videos supporting the uprising. Some social media campaigns popularized designated hashtags by utilizing a number of high-profile accounts such as US singer Rihanna (@rihanna, 2019) and British model Naomi Campbell (@naomi, 2019). These messages on social media were successful in raising awareness for the movement and in prompting discussion on the hashtag and, therefore, on the revolution.

On June 30, 2019, huge numbers of protestors took to the streets in many cities across the country—despite an Internet blackout—stressing demands for freedom, peace and equality (Abdullah et al., 2019). The massive protest forced the TMC to accept mediation from the African Union and the Ethiopian government leading a deal between the MTC and the FFC. The deal led to a creation of a joint military and civilian Sovereignty Council that assumed power on August, 20, 2019.

This study builds on the work of Hollyer et al. (2015), Howard (2011) and Kalathil and Boas (2003). Arguments presented by these scholars suggest that online access to previously concealed political, social, or economic news in non-democratic countries, could raise general discontent and create social unrest that would destabilize autocratic regimes. Their research provides insights and theoretical underpinnings suggesting that policies of the Sudanese government could have affected the protesters' online news consumption and eventually influenced the magnitude of their protest participation. To examine these contentions, the study poses a number of research questions and asks an important segment of the protesters to tell their stories.

Method

The narratives used in this chapter came from the interviews of the people who participated in the uprising in December 2018. The sample for this qualitative study included 20 participants: 10 male and 10 female college students. To collect information about college students' social media use during the Sudanese uprising, I used the snowballing and networking technique to get a representative sample in terms of age, gender and college (Cresswell, 2012). The age of the participants ranged from 17 to 26 years old. All the interviewees used social media, participated and lived the experience of the December 2018 uprising. The 20 participants contributed their ideas and shared their lived experiences in in-depth interviews (Edwards & Holland, 2013). The questions were open-ended allowing the participants to speak their minds. Prompts, probes and laddering techniques were used to gain as much insight as possible from participants. All interviews were conducted in person and recorded after obtaining participants' consent. The interviewees were assured of the anonymity and confidentiality of the information they shared. Pseudonyms were used for all identifying information to ensure participant confidentiality. All of the interviews were conducted in Arabic. The interviews were transcribed, translated into English, and thematically analyzed (Cresswell, 2013).

Findings

Social Media Helped Protestors in Raising Political Awareness

Most of the interviewees referred the government control of television and radio channels as well as strict censorship of newspapers. They suggested that raising political awareness required alternative media which they found in social media. Many interviewees asserted that social media played a big role in the uprising. "Social media played a big role in the revolution by raising political awareness internally and externally" (Sami, a 19-year-old male). A number of stories about the government's brutality and torture of political prisoners were shared on social media. Kamil, a 20-year-old male, argued: "Personally, social media helped me knew political parties that I did not know before. Also the torture houses, I did not know they existed." Government forces committed numerous stories of government atrocities against civilian populations in Darfur. Mona asserted: "there were many inhumane things happening in Darfur that we did not know." Some people publicize stories of injustice and their grievances and people sympathize with them (Aya). Maryam argued: "For example if we make a symposium very few people would attend, and the security may use tear gas to disperse it. But on social media we could avoid that." Using social media to raise political awareness about the injustices that the government committed motivated many people to join the protests against the government.

Some interviewees suggested that social media did not play a big role in the uprising.

> Social media did not play a big role in raising political awareness because the revolution started because of the economic crisis and later became political. But the real reason was the living of the people. . . . People used to queue from the Dawn prayer and for long hours to get bread.
>
> (Sharif, a 24-year-old male)

Social Media Helped in Mobilizing Protests

All the interviewees underscored the importance of social media in helping the protesters mobilize people to participate in the demonstrations. Aya noted: "Communication sites have greatly helped in organizing and political mobilization. Without social networking sites there would not have been this large gathering." "Before you go out of your home, you know that these people were attacked (*Ballohom*) so we go to another place. Social media helped people to stay safe and allowed people to know where they are going and how to connect people to each other" (Sarah). The government also tried to mobilize its supporters to defuse the protests. Ahmed argued that "There was mobilization and counter mobilization. The SPA's page played a big role and effective role."

Social Media Facilitated Coordination During Protests

Coordinating protesters activities on the streets was instrumental to the success of the uprising. All the interviewees agreed that social media played a crucial role in helping the protesters coordinate the protests. Sharif argued: "The SPA's page played an important role in organizing the protests. If there were guests from revolutionaries among them, the Resistance Committees used to protect the guests in their houses." Resistance Committees played important roles in organizing demonstrations in the districts including Ombadda, in Omdurman. "Their message was easy to understand because it was in local Arabic compared to the complicated messages of the SPA which were in formal Standard Arabic" (Ali). The same sentiments were expressed by Sarah, who asserted: "Without social media reach I don't think the numbers of the people participating would be that huge. The role of the SPA's page was great. It provided the people with the schedules and places of protests." Sharing information on social media was instrumental in coordinating the movements of the demonstrators. For example, when the people took to the streets on 6 April, social media informed them that there would be a sit-in and they should be unified. This could not have happened without social media (Zahra). Social media also enabled the protesters to share their experiences when encounter security forces. In some situations, they have to deal with live ammunition, and in other instances, they have to endure tear gas and beatings. Mona added:

> Social media was used to tell people how to deal with tear gas and to show citizens how to use leaves of *Neem* trees to wipe their faces. Without social networking sites, people would not know how to deal with tear gas.

Social Media Enabled Protesters to Inform the World About What Was Happening in Sudan

The protesters knew that social media was beyond the control of the Sudanese government. Kamil contended, "Social media succeeded in informing the world about what had happened in the Sudan. There were many protests around the world who expressed support for the Sudanese revolution." One respondent referred to positive role of Radio Dabanga and the pages of SPA and Resistance Committees as "the voice of the Sudanese Revolution . . . and an alternative to the Ministry of Information" (Mona).

Salah, a 20-year-old male, argued:

> Social media help substantially in conveying what was happening in the Sudan to the outside world. We find protesters in Algeria, Palestine, and Lebanon emulating what had happened in the Sudan. Even in the USA, BLM benefited from tactics of Sudanese protesters.

Nazik asserted:

> Social media helped in extending the breadth of publicity. For example Facebook was very instrumental and enabled the revolutionaries to inform the world about what was happening in the Sudan. It was terrific to see TV channels like *al-Jazeera*, *Al-Arabeya*, and *Al-Haddath* broadcasting news from the Sudan. The reporters of these channels were very active and they got their information from the social media particularly the Facebook.

The respondents highlighted the instrumental role of the activists' activities on Twitter. Salah argued: "Hashtag #Blu4Sudan, about martyr Mattar attracted huge interactions although many people abroad did not know the geographical place of Sudan on the map. Without social media the world would not have known that we have a revolution . . . #Blu4Sudan became a trend" (Mona).

Social Media Helped in Refuting the Government's Narratives

Most of the respondents agreed that social media enabled the protesters to challenge the government's narratives and refute them. Salah argued:

> For example, the government representatives were saying "there were no demonstrations" on *Al-Hadath* channel. The revolutionaries responded by posting videos showing the streets barricaded (*Matarssah*) and blocked.

Social media helped refute the government's narrative. "Some people were deceived and believed the government's story about the terrorist plot of the Darfurian students. But, social media helped refute that allegation" (Samy, a 19-year-old male). On the other hand, another respondent asserted that social media did not play a big role in refuting the government's messages "because no one believed these messages. Many people used to believe the SPA, although some people discredited it" (Ahmed, a 25-year-old male). Sarah, a 20-year-old female, added:

> Whenever someone from "Jadad Electrony" (E-Chickens) writes fake news or something that did not happen, immediately people respond to him/her and correct the information instantly. The revolutionaries succeeded to large extent in refuting misinformation and rumors.

The majority of the respondents indicated that the Sudanese people believed the protesters' messages because "there was evidence including audio and video coupled with live broadcast" (Mona). Although broadcast media and print media were directly or indirectly controlled by the government, they failed to substantiate the government's messages. Zahra, a 21-year-old female, argued:

> The people used to make fun of their speech using a comic song in a video clip. The people did not take their messages seriously because they were laughing stock. For example, whenever Bashir makes a speech he starts singing and dancing. He used to speak disdainfully and represented the pinnacle of disrespect for the Sudanese people. The people responded with the same token.

The Government's Reaction to the Protesters' Activities

Having in mind the dominant of young men and women in the Sudanese uprising, it is expected that young protesters will carry out most of the online anti-government activities. Although the government hired communication experts and established what was known as Electronic Battalions (*Katayib Electroniah*), the protesters supported by anti-governments abroad succeeded in dominating battle in cyberspace. According to Samy, "The government used violent methods against the revolutionaries using networks, and it used to target activists and used immoral methods against them." Salah, a 20-year-old male, argued:

> Bashir derided the protesters as "*Shozaz Afaq*"(narrow-minded), and cited Holy Quran informing a police rally "مكلو في صاصقلا دايق"(and for you in retribution there is a life). We interpreted that as a signal to police and security organs to kill the protesters. The government could not reach the activists like Za al-Noon in Malaysia.

The government also managed to use Photoshop and video editing techniques and doctored old videos to portray big protests as small protests (Ahmed). Moreover, the government reacted by blocking Facebook, WhatsApp and the Internet. Ali noted, "the government used the '*Electronic Battalions*' which the people nicknamed '*Jidad Electrony*.' Their role was to send out rumors and support the government stories." The same ideas were repeated by a number of respondents. Zainab, a 21-year-old female, asserted:

> The government used fake accounts and *Dajaj Electrony* (Electronic Chickens) to spread rumors and say that *Katayib Dhil* (Shadow Battalions) will disperse the Sit-in by force so as to scare people and make them leave.

Another respondent described the government's response as "very provocative." Nazik added:

> The government talked about "Shadow Battalions that you know very well." This language encouraged more people to protest. They arrested the activists and their followers, and shave the hair of young men who they called communists. This cruel treatment motivated many people to participate in the protests.

Many respondents were outraged by the government's depictions of protesters and framing of the uprising. In the words of Basmah, a 18-year-old female, "They depicted the protestors as tramps (*Sa'aleyq*) and homeless street boys (*Shammasha*) who are good for nothing." Another respondent concurred and added, "the government said there were traitors, mercenaries, and deviants who want the country to plunge in a chaotic situation" (Maryam, a 17-year-old female)

The Government Cut off the Internet to Hide the Crime

All the respondents agreed that the government resorted to Internet blackout to prevent the protesters from exchanging information and exposing the crimes that the military committed during the forcible dispersal of the sit-in. Sharif, a 24-year-old male, argued, "The main reason was that the government did not want the world to see what had happened during the dispersal of sit-in." Some respondents argued that the government wanted to hide the perpetrators of the crimes committed during the brutal dispersal of the sit-in. One respondent suggested that the government "proved that they committed the crime" (Adam). They blocked the Internet to stop the spread of the news about the dispersal of the sit-in, and thus, according to Samy, "The government did not want the people to know the identity of those who dispersed the sit-in so that the issue remains unknown. According to Zainab, "The government made the Internet blackout to stop the spread of information about the people who were killed, lost, and injured. They don't want news of the massacre to go out."

Sarah added, "they disconnected the Internet because the people were starting to organize on the social media. If they allowed social media during that time of public outrage, massive protests could have happened on the streets." Another respondent added, "Al-Bashir's government cut off the Internet because most of the people were documenting the facts, and they were transmitting live broadcast to satellite channels" (Mona).

In the absence of the Internet and social media, the protesters used alternative media to communicate and exchange information about what had happened during the horrendous dispersal of the sit-in. Aya, a 18-year-old female, argued, "The alternatives that the revolutionaries used, including VPNs, SMS messages, and VPNs on *Canar* and *Sudani* SIM cards." According to one respondent, available media included Voice of the Revolution, *Radio Dabanga*, in addition to telephone conversations (Mona).

Despite the Internet blackout, "the revolutionaries" continued to communicate using "telephone conversation and word-of-mouth to hold secret meeting to organize protests" (Nazik). The protesters also used paper clips, printouts, graffiti and murals, and they expressed their discontent by burning tires on the streets. One respondent asserted that the Internet blackout did not stop the uprising arguing, "The fact that the people succeeded in protesting in the millions of June 30 was an evidence that the Internet blackout was not a problem" (Nazik).

One respondent argued, "It was in the interest of the civilians to continue the sit-in and not to disperse it because it was a bargaining chip to exert pressure on the military to form a civilian government." Maryam added:

> But the sit-in was dispersed after the agreement between some parties and the military. The puzzling question is why the sit-in was dispersed? May be the two sides agreed that they could not meet the demands of the youth. Two years passed and we don't know who dispersed the sit-in and no one become accountable for that.

Social Media Contributed Considerably to the Sudanese Uprising

The majority of the interviewees agreed that social media contributed immensely to the success of the uprising. Some of them claimed that the uprising could not have happened without the use of social media. Mona, a 19-year-old female, claimed:

> The December revolution could not have happened without social media because of the information blackout. Social media was our source of information. Without it the revolution could have died and no one could have known about it.

A similar note was echoed by Zainab who argued that "I mean, people say to you, the old people used to say that you are a few brazen people. Using social media, we were able to communicate with each other. If we did not create the family of the social media, the revolution could not have succeeded." Ahmed concurred and added:

> Without Social media the revolution could not have succeeded. During previous revolutions the people had had political awareness, but during the *Kaizan* 30 years in power they did not allow political organizations. Moreover, lifting the subsidies from necessary goods added to the problem.

Some respondents highlighted the diplomatic isolation of the Sudanese government in the international arena. One respondent asserted: "I think the *Inghaz* leaders are indicted globally for war crimes they had had to remain in power even after removing Bashir. The revolution could not have happened without Social media" (Ali, a 23-year-old male).

Other interviewees appreciated the importance of social media and argued that the uprising could have succeeded without it. These two groups referred to the Sudanese government's control over traditional and hailed social media for enabling them to communicate, mobilize and coordinate protests. Aya argued:

> New voices of young women appeared like *Kandaka* Ala Salah, and Rifqa, the tear gas cans' "Hunter." Many young people were able to convey their experiences to the people through social media.

Another interviewee added: "To some extent, the revolution could not have succeeded without social media. Social media helped them in knowing the places of the protests" (Sharif). Rising cost of living and deterioration of public education and healthcare sector motivated many people to join the protests. Adam, a 26-year-old male, argued: "The revolution could have succeeded without social media because the people were suffering when they took to the streets. But Social media helped by saving them time and effort."

Other four female respondents agreed that it played a very big role in the "revolution" because it gave people a "voice" and allowed them to stand together.

Some respondents argued that the uprising could have succeeded without social media. They cited atrocities of the Sudanese government against protesters in the past, economic hardship, and the deteriorating living conditions. Kamil argued:

> The revolution could have succeeded even without social media, because if there is a will goals could be achieved." A second interviewee concurred arguing that: The revolution could have succeeded without social media because there were many revolutions succeeded without them.

Nazik, a 23-year-old female interviewee, added:

> Social media helped in moving the people. But, in addition to social media, many people became fed up with government and the pain of those killed in Sept. 2013 protests was still lingering in the hearts of the people. Because of that and the grievances, the revolution could have succeeded without the Social media.

Resistance Committees in many Sudanese towns work locally at the residential level. Anti-government activists get to know each other and communicated using telephones, face-to-face communication and word-of-mouth. Maryam contended:

> We in Jabra [southern Khartoum] Resistance Committees we used to communicate without the Internet because we develop good relations and were able to organize processions without the Internet. It was not easy but we did it.

Discussion

Social media provided an unpresented opportunity to the Sudanese protesters. They have no other way to communicate and share ideas because all mass media organizations are controlled by the government. But the role of social media should be understood in context. The Internet access in the country was limited. Western-educated and liberal Sudanese succeeded in conveying the protesters' demands for freedom, peace and equality to the outside world through Facebook, Twitter, YouTube and Instagram. It is worth noting that their influence on global public opinion could hardly be translated into concrete success inside the country. Western audiences may perceive online sentiments expressed by these elitist and liberal groups on social media as representative of the hearts and minds of the majority of the Sudanese people.

While the Internet penetration was limited and social media use was extremely important in qualitative rather than quantitative terms. Some activists succeeded in taking online messages to the people on the streets using printouts, flyers, murals, songs and word-of-mouth (Hollyer et al., 2015; Coffé, 2017). Social media was indeed a catalyst for the raising awareness and coordination during the protests (Rane & Salem, 2012). Moreover, social media, in the words of most of the respondents, represented an alternative media enabling the protesters to challenge the government narrative on traditional media and set the protesters' agendas (Cottle, 2011; Kirkizh & Koltsova, 2021). Many respondents were pleased that satellite channels such as *Al-Jazeera*, *Al-Arabeya* and *Al-Hadath* used some of the information that the protesters posted on social media. Such a multi-step flow of information enabled many people who could not afford to buy expensive smartphones to watch news about the uprising on satellite television.

The interviewees highlighted the importance of social media in raising political awareness, mobilization and coordinating the protests (Loader et al., 2016; Herrera, 2014; Eltantawy & Wiest, 2011). They paid tribute to the SPA as well as the Resistance Committees for their online and offline contributions during the uprising. Most of the interviewees agreed that the SPA played a primary role in setting the schedules and paths of the demonstrations. They also appreciated the knowledge and experience of the Resistance Committees, which were perceived as closer to the ordinary person on the street compared to the SPA.

Cognizant of the government grip over traditional media, the interviewees presented arguments highlighting the importance of social media use in informing the outside world about what was happening in the Sudan during the uprising. Many of the interviewees referred to the positive coverage of Arab satellite channels, namely *Al-Jazeera*, *Al-Arabeya* and *Al-Haddath*. The comments described these channels as fair in their coverage because, on many occasions, these channels relied on the information that the protesters post on social media (Miladi, 2016). The majority of the interviewees argued that such a coverage was instrumental in helping them reach many audiences inside Sudan and abroad. The interviewees believed that social media had helped them voice their grievances, inform the world and challenge the government's narratives. Some interviewees recalled a broadcast by the government describing the killing of a young protester. The government said the victim was killed by a female protester who was carrying a gun in her handbag. The story was refuted and described by activists as "bizarre story." None of the interviewees referred to the agendas of these channels, their financiers and their impact on the Sudan as a sovereign state.

The government reacted by pushing back and managed to overcome the challenges that the protesters launched on social media. This gives credit to arguments posed by some scholars who challenged the notion depicting as a democratizing (Morozov, 2012). The Sudanese government online activities were conducted by pro-government forces named Electronic Battalions. Thus, the Internet and social media have enabled post-Bashir government to expand its repression and authoritarian rule (Nisbet & Meyers, 2010; Lynch, 2011). Nonetheless, the protesters found alternative means to circumvent governmental surveillance by using word-of-mouth, landline telephones, as well as VPN proxies.

While many of the interviewees argued that the use of social media is a boon for positive development enhancing positive social change, it is important to note that the Sudanese government also utilized social media to discredit the activists and diffuse the protests. During the uprising, the Sudanese government sent out numerous video and text messages on Facebook, Twitter and YouTube to disarm its opponents and stabilize the situation

(Curran et al., 2012). The security organs detained some activists and managed to block their online activities. The government responded harshly during the sit-in in front of the General Headquarters of the Military Forces by cutting off the Internet enforcing a total information blackout. The brutal dispersal of the sit-in and communication blackout deterred many people from taking to the streets. Nonetheless, some people found ways to bypass government controlled media and managed to reach their audiences at home and abroad using proxies and landline telephones.

The interviewees emphatically described the Internet blackout as a premeditated act to prevent the protesters from sharing images and videos of atrocities committed by the military during the dispersal of the sit-in with the outside world. They argued that knowing about the crimes and watching the graphic videos of repression and killings could have motivated many people to take to the streets against the government (Yousef & Nafisa, 2019). In this respect, some of the interviewees suggested that the government tactic had succeeded in diffusing the momentum of rage and anger that followed the brutal dispersal of the sit-in.

Conclusion

The Sudanese government's control over print and broadcast media has been challenged by the advent of social media. The government protesters use of social media has posed a threat to the government's dominance in private and public space. An authoritarian regime could no longer exercise full control over the flow of information and the framing of news. Most of the respondents praised social media as an enabling instrument for facilitating mass mobilization and coordinating activities during protests. Interestingly, none of the interviewees mentioned the digital divide and inability of the majority of the Sudanese to access the Internet and use social media. Nonetheless, they expressed divergent opinions on the potency of social media in communicative act and social change. While some of the interviews asserted that the uprising could not have happened without social media, a few of them argued that the uprising could have happened without social media. Some respondents asserted the uprising could have happened without social media, but with a lesser speed and efficiency. Post-uprising events proved that the government succeeded in buying time and was able to infiltrate the activists and weaken them. Protesters and activists became aware of the fact that successful campaigns in cyberspace may not translate into tangible success in reality.

To achieve the goals of the uprising and make the dream of freedom, peace and equality come true, it requires hard work among the general population. Refuting official narratives does not necessarily mean persuading the people with alternative counter-narratives. Elitist narratives should rub shoulders with what is on the mind of an ordinary person on the street. Social media can be extremely effective in raising awareness and mobilizing like-minded educated protesters, but may not be very effective in rallying ordinary people at the grassroots level. That is the critical mass required for creating any viable social change. Subsequent events have proven that the momentum of the uprising was upheld by many activists in diaspora and few protesters at home. Religious, sectarian and tribal leaders remain popular public figures. Islamic opinion leaders affiliated with the government have easy access to public radio and television stations. At various occasions, the government relied on their influence to support official policies and overcome civil unrest. Political opponents used the internet and social media to express their opinions, voice their concerns and mobilize followers against the government. Information and communication technologies may not be a panacea for a developing country struggling to overcome the woes of structural adjustment programs. Top-down approaches and attempts aimed at using ICT for development and democratization will face the same fate as older modernization paradigms.

The Sudanese experience has shown that social media has had a disruptive effect on the government's dominance in the public sphere. Nonetheless, they did not create a viable alternative to populate that sphere with civilian, free, peaceful and equitable democratic rule. On the other hand, the government used social media to exert control over opponents through surveillance, harassment, or outright Internet blackout. Thus, social media can act as an interactive communication tool for creating a flourishing democracy or maintaining autocratic rule and repression. The government and its opponents will continue their struggle using social media to serve their competing narratives in cyberspace.

This exploratory study has a number of limitations. One limitation is the composition of the sample. Future research should aim at recruiting respondents from different age groups as well as professional and working groups. The qualitative method can be complemented by a quantitative sample to achieve more representation. More research is needed on sources as well as the content of messages on social media. Content analysis can provide important insights into message design and strategy. Future research is required to show the role of social media in intermedia agenda-setting and the effects resulting from the convergence of messages across various media platforms.

References

Abdullah, Y., al-Taher, N. & Khadder, K. (2019). At Least 7 Dead as Tens of Thousands Protest in Sudan, Demanding Civilian Rule. [Online] Available at: https://edition.cnn.com/2019/06/30/africa/sudan-mass-protest-intl/index.html
Abushouk, A. (2021). Al-Thawra al-Sudaniyya (2018–2019): Muqaraba tawthiqiya-tahliliya li dawafi'eha wa Marahiliha wa tahadaiyatiha [The Sudanese revolution

(2018–2019): A documentary and analytical approach to its goals, stages and challenges]. *Doha, Qatar: Arab Center for Research & Policy Studies.*

Albaih, K. (2015, October 15). How WhatsApp is fueling a "sharing revolution" in Sudan. *The Guardian.* www.theguardian.com/world/2015/oct/15/sudan-whatsapp-sharing-revolution

Ali, N. M. (2019). Sudanese women's groups on Facebook and #Civil_Disobedience: Nairat or Thairat? (Radiant or revolutionary?). *African Studies Review, 62*(2), 103–126.

Avril, K., & Melis, G. (2017). Social media and youth political engagement: Preaching to the converted or providing a new voice for youth? *The British Journal of Politics and International Relations, 19*(4). Available at https://journals.sagepub.com/doi/10.1177/1369148117718461

BBC News Arabic (2018). #Mudun_al-Sudan_Tantafid lil yawm al-θani ḥasidatu qatla wa jarḥa. [Online] Available at: https://www.bbc.com/arabic/trending-46632086

BBC News. (2019). *Sudan coup leader Awad Ibn auf steps down.* Retrieved September 17, 2022, from www.bbc.com/news/world-africa-47913338

Bellin, E. (2012). Reconsidering the robustness of authoritarianism in the middle east: Lessons from the Arab Spring. *Comparative Politics, 44*(2), 127–149.

Bendimerad, R., & Faisal, N. (2019). *#BlueforSudan: Why is social media turning blue for Sudan?* Retrieved October 25, 2022, from www.aljazeera.com/news/2019/06/blueforsudan-social-media-turning-blue-sudan-190613132528243.html

Berridge, W. J. (2019). Briefing: The uprising in Sudan. *African Affairs, 119*(474), 1–13.

Bodrunova, S. S., & Litvinenko, A. A. (2013). New media and the political protest: The formation of a public counter-sphere in Russia, 2008–12. In A. Makarychev & A. Mommen (Eds.), *Russia's changing economic and political regimes: The Putin years and afterwards* (pp. 29–66). Routledge.

Breuer, A. (2016). The role of social media in mobilizing political protest: Evidence from the Tunisian revolution. In E. A. Sayre & T. M Yousef (Eds.), *Young generation awakening: Economics, society, and policy on the eve of the Arab spring* (pp. 110–131). Oxford University Press.

Brundidge, J., Garrett, K. R., Rojas, H., & de Zúñiga, H. G. (2014). Political participation and ideological news online: Differential gains and differential losses in a presidential election cycle. *Mass Communication and Society,* 17, 464–486.

Brym, R., Godbout, M., Hoffbauer, A., Menard, G., & Zhang, T. H. (2014). Social media in the 2011 Egyptian uprising. *The British Journal of Sociology, 65*(2), 266–292.

Burke, J. (2019). *The guardian: Sudan protestors reject army takeover after removal of president.* Retrieved October 15, 18, 2022, from https://www.theguardian.com/world/2019/apr/11/sudan-army-ousts-bashir-after-30-years-in-power

Castells, M. (2012). *Networks of outrage and hope: Social movements in the Internet age.* Polity Press.

Chan, M. (2017). Media use and the social identity model of collective action: Examining the roles of online alternative news and social media news. *Journalism & Mass Communication Quarterly, 94*(3), 663–681.

Coffé, H. (2017). Citizens' media use and the accuracy of their perceptions of electoral integrity. *International Political Science Review, 38*(3), 281–297.

Comunello, F., & Anzera, G. (2012). Will the revolution be tweeted? A conceptual frame-work for understanding the social media and the Arab Spring. *Islam and Christian–Muslim Relations, 23*(4), 453–470.

Copnall, J. (2013). *BBC news: Sudan feels the heat from fuel protests*. Retrieved November 10, 2022, from www.bbc.com/news/world-africa-24938224

Cottle, S. (2011). Media and the Arab uprisings of 2011: Research notes. *Journalism, 12*(5), 647–659. doi:10.1177/1464884911410017

Couldry, N. (2013, November 21). *A necessary disenchantment: Myth, agency and injustice in the digital age*. Inaugural Lecture, London School of Economics.

Couldry, N., Livingstone, S., & Markham, T. (2016). *Media consumption and public engagement: Beyond the presumption of attention*. Springer.

Creswell, J. W. (2013). *Qualitative Inquiry and research design choosing among five approaches* (3rd ed.). Sage Publications.

Curran, J., Fenton, N., & Freedman, D. (2012). *Misunderstanding the internet*. Routledge.

Downey, N., & Fenton, J. (2003). Counter public spheres and global modernity. *Journal of the European Institute for Communication and Culture*. Javnost—The Public, *10*(1), 15–32. https://doi.org/10.1080/13183222.2003.11008819

Dutta, N., & Bhat, A. (2016). *Use of social media for political engagement: A literature review*. Retrieved November 8, 2022, from www.aims-international.org/aims14/14acd/PDF/A226-Final.pdf

Earl, J., & Kimport, K. (2011). *Digitally enabled social change: Activism in the internet age (acting with technology)*. MIT Press.

Edwards, R., & Holland, J. (2013). *What is qualitative interviewing?* A&C Black. Retrieved from http://eprints.ncrm.ac.uk/3276/1/complete_proofs.pdf

Elmileik, A., & Khalil, S. (2019). *"Tasgut bas" to #SudanUprising: How social media told the story*. Retrieved October 25, 2022, from www.aljazeera.com/features/2019/8/12/tasgut-bas-to-sudanuprising-how-social-media-told-the-story

Eltantawy, N., & Wiest, J. (2011). Social media in the Egyptian revolution: Reconsidering resource mobilization theory. *International Journal of Communication, 5*, 1207–1224.

Eltigani, E. (n.a). *Sudan mediascape*. Retrieved November 10, 2022, from https://media landscapes.org/country/sudan

Enikolopov, R., Makarin, A., & Petrova, M. (2020). Social media and protest participation: Evidence from Russia. *Econometrica, 88*(4), 1479–1514.

Faris, D., (2013). *Dissent and revolution in a digital age: Social media, blogging and activism in Egypt*. Palgrave Macmillan.

Feezell, J. T. (2016). Predicting online political participation. The importance of selection bias and selective exposure in the online setting. *Political Research Quarterly, 69*(3), 495–509.

Fuchs, C. (2010). Alternative media as critical media. *European Journal of Social Theory, 13*(2), 173–192.

Galander, M. (2021). Sudan: Media under the military–democratic pendulum. In C. Richter & C. Kozman (Eds.), *Arab media systems* (pp. 233–247). Open Book Publishers. https://doi.org/10.11647/OBP.0238

Garrett, R. K. (2006). Protest in an information society: A review of literature on social movements and new ICTs. *Information, Communication and Society, 9*(2), 202–224. doi:10.1080/13691180600630773

Gerbaudo, P. (2012). *Tweets and the streets: Social media and contemporary activism*. Pluto Press.

Habermas, J. (1989 [1991]). *The structural transformation of the public sphere: An inquiry into a category of bourgeois society* (T. Burger, Trans.). MIT Press.

Habermas, J. (2006). Political communication in media society: Does democracy still enjoy an epistemic dimension? The impact of normative theory on empirical research. *Communication Theory, 16*, 411–426.

Habermas, J., Lennox, S., & Lennox, F. (1974). The public sphere: An encyclopedia article (1964). *New German Critique, 3*, 49–55.

Hale, S. (2014). The new middle east insurrections and other subversions of the modernist frame. *Journal of Middle East Women's Studies, 10*(3), 40–61.

Hall, S. (1991). Encoding/decoding. In D. Hobson, A. Lowe, P. Willis, & S. Hall (Eds.), *Culture, media, language: Working papers in cultural studies, 1972–79* (pp. 117–127). London: Routledge.

Hall, S. (2003). Encoding/decoding. In S. Hall, D. Lowe, & P. Willis (Eds.), *Culture, media, language* (pp. 127–137). Routledge.

Hassanpour, N. (2014). Media disruption and revolutionary unrest: Evidence from Mubarak's quasi-experiment. *Political Communication, 31*(1), 1–24.

Herrera, L. (2014). *Revolution in the age of social media: The Egyptian popular insurrection and the internet.* Verso.

Hofheinz, A. (2017). Broken walls: Challenges to patriarchal authority in the eyes of Sudanese social media actors. *Die Welt des Islams, 57*(3–4), 278–302.

Hollyer, R. J., Rosendorff, P. B., & Vreeland, J. R. (2015). Transparency, protest, and autocratic instability. *American Political Science Review, 109*(4), 764–784.

Howard, P. N. (2011). *Digital origins of dictatorship and democracy: Information technology and political Islam.* Oxford University Press.

Howard, P. N., & Hussain, M. (2013). *Democracy's fourth wave? Digital media and the Arab Spring.* Oxford University Press.

Kalathil, S., & Boas, T. C. (2003). *Open networks, closed regimes: The impact of the internet on authoritarian rule.* Carnegie Endowment for International Peace.

Karatzogianni, A. (2015). The social media political subject is an infant. *Social Media + Society, 1*(1). https://doi.org/10.1177/2056305115580480

Keating, A., & Melis, G. (2017a). Social media and youth political engagement: Preaching to the converted or providing a new voice for youth? *The British Journal of Politics and International Relations, 19*(4), 877–894.

Keating, A., & Melis, G. (2017b). Social media and youth political engagement: Preaching to the converted or providing a new voice for youth? *The British Journal of Politics and International Relation, 19*(4), 877–894.

Keck, M. E., & Sikkink, K. (2014). *Activists beyond borders: Advocacy networks in international politics.* Cornell University Press.

Kim, Y., & Amnå, E. (2015). Internet use and political engagement in youth. In J. Coleman & D. Freelon (Eds.), *Handbook of digital politics* (pp. 221–243). Edward Elgar Publishing.

Kirkizh, N., & Koltsova, O. (2021, January–March). Online news and protest participation in a political context: Evidence from self-reported cross-sectional data. *Social Media + Society*, 1–10.

Kruse, L. M., Norris, D. R., Jonathan, R., & Flinchum, J. R. (2018). Social media as a public sphere? Politics on social media. *The Sociological Quarterly, 59*(1), 62–84. https://doi.org/10.1080/00380253.2017.1383143

Ladd, M. J., & Lenz, G. S. (2009). Exploiting a rare communication shift to document the persuasive power o Little, T. A. (2015). Communication technology and protest. *Journal of Politics, 78*(1), 152–166.

Leung, D. K. K., & Lee, F. L. F. (2014). Cultivating an active online counterpublic: Examining usage and political impact of internet alternative media. *The International Journal of Press/ Politics, 19*, 340–359.

Lim, M. (2012). Clicks, cabs, and coffee houses: Social media and oppositional movements in Egypt 2004–2011. *Journal of Communication, 62*, 231–248.

Loader, B. D., Vromen, A., & Xenos, M. A. (2016). Performing for the young networked citizen? Celebrity politics, social networking and the political engagement of young people. *Media, Culture & Society, 38*(3), 400–419.

Lorentzen, P. (2014). China's strategic censorship. *American Journal of Political Science, 58*(2), 402–414.

Lotan, G., Graeff, E., Ananny, M., Gaffney, D., Pearce, I., & Boyd, d. (2011). The revolutions were tweeted: Information flows during the 2011 Tunisian and Egyptian revolutions. *International Journal of Communication, 5*, 1375–1405.theo

Lovink, G. (2019). *Sad by design: On platform nihilism.* Pluto Press. Retrieved October 2, 2022, from www.jstor.org/stable/j.ctvg8p6dv.7

Lynch, M. (2003). Beyond the Arab Street: Iraq and the Arab Public Sphere. *Politics & Society, 31*(1), 55–91.

Lynch, M. (2011). After Egypt: The Limits and Promise of Online Challenges to the Authoritarian Arab State. *Perspective on Politics, 9*(2), 301–310.

Malik, N. (2019). *The military crackdown in Sudan lays bare the dark heart of Bashir's regime.* Retrieved November 10, 2022, from www.theguardian.com/ commentisfree/2019/jun/04/military-sudan-bashir-protesters-death-khartoum

McDonald, P., & Thompson, P. (2016). Social media (tion) and the reshaping of public/ private boundaries in employment relations. *International Journal of Management Reviews, 18*(1), 69–84.

Meirowitz, A., & Tucker, J. (2013). People power or a one-shot deal? A dynamic model of protest. *American Journal of Political Science, 57*(2), 478–490.

Middle East Eye (2019). Sudan: The Names of 100 People Killed in a Week of Deadly Violence. [Online] Available at: https://www.middleeasteye.net/news/sudan-names-100-killed-deadly-week

Miladi, N. (2016). Social media and social change. *Digest of Middle East Studies, 25*(1), 36–51.

Morozov, E. (2012). *The net delusion: The dark side of internet freedom.* Public Affairs.

Musa, B. A. (2014). Twitter and Tahrir square: Social media and the Arab spring uprising. In B. A. Musa & J. Willis (Eds.). *From Twitter to Tahrir square: Ethics in social and new media communication* (pp. 265–275). Praeger.

Nisbet, Erik C., & Myers, Teresa A. (2010). Challenging the state: Transnational TV and political identity in the middle east. *Political Communication, 27*(4), 347–366.

Norris, P. (2012, April). *The impact of social media on the Arab uprisings: The Facebook, Twitter, and YouTube revolutions?* Paper presented at Advancing Comparative Political Communication Research: New Frameworks, Designs and Data, European Consortium Joint Workshops.

Oser, J., Hooghe, M., & Marien, S. (2013). Is online participation distinct from offline participation? A latent class analysis of participation types and their stratification. *Political Research Quarterly, 66*(1), 91–101.

Patrick, A. (2019). *Al-Jazeera: Why social media is going blue for Sudan?* Retrieved October 24, 2022, from https://edition.cnn.com/2019/06/13/africa/sudan-social-media-campaign-intl/index.html

Rane, H., & Salem, S. (2012). Social media, social movements and the diffusion of ideas in the Arab uprisings. *Journal of International Communication, 18*(1), 97–111. doi:10.1080/13216597.2012.662168

Reuter, O. J., & Szakonyi, D. (2015). Online social media and political awareness in authoritarian regimes. *British Journal of Political Science, 45*(1), 29–51.

Schlozman, K. L., Verba, S., & Brady, H. E. (2012). *The unheavenly chorus: Unequal political voice and the broken promise of American democracy.* Princeton University Press.

Statcounter. (2019). *Social media Stats Sudan.* Retrieved November 10, 2022, from https://gs.statcounter.com/social-media-stats/all/sudan/#monthly-201901-201903-bar

Tang, M., & Huhe, N. (2014). Alternative framing: The effect of the internet on political support in authoritarian China. *International Political Science Review, 35*(5), 559–576.

Theocharis, Y., & Lowe, W. (2016). Does Facebook increase political participation? Evidence from a field experiment. *Information, Communication and Society, 19*(10), 1465–1486.

Theocharis, Y., Lowe, W., Van Deth, J. W., et al. (2015). Using Twitter to mobilize protest action: Online mobilization patterns and action repertoires in the Occupy Wall Street, Indignados, and Aganaktismenoi movements. *Information, Communication & Society, 18*(2), 202–220.

Theocharis, Y., & Quintelier, E. (2014). Stimulating citizenship or expanding entertainment? The effect of Facebook on adolescent participation. *New Media & Society,* (18), 817–836.

Tufekci, Z., & Wilson, C. (2012). Social media and the decision to participate in political protest: Observations from Tahrir square. *Journal of Communication, 62,* 363–379.

UNDP, Khartoum Office. (2019). *Making sense of social media proxies: Findings of social media study on Sudan.* Available at https://www.undp.org/africa/publications/making-sense-social-media-proxies-sudan

Valenzuela, S., Arriagada, A., & Scherman, A. (2012). The social media basis of youth protest behavior: The case of Chile. *Journal of Communication, 62,* 299–314.

Vissers, S., Hooghe, M., Stolle, D., & Maheo, V.-A. (2012). The impact of mobilization media on off-line and online participation: Are mobilization effects medium-specific? *Social Science Computer Review, 30*(2), 152–169.

Wilson, C., & Dunn, A. (2011). Digital media in the Egyptian revolution: Descriptive analysis from the Tahrir data sets. *International Journal of Communication, 5,* 1248–1272.

Wojcieszak, M., Bimber, B., Feldman, L., & Stroud, N. J. (2016). Partisan news and political participation: Exploring mediated relationships. *Political Communication, 33*(2), 241–260.

Wolfsfeld, G., Segev, E., & Sheafer, T. (2013). Social media and the Arab spring politics comes first. *The International Journal of Press/Politics, 18,* 115–137.

Woodstock, L. (2016). "It's kind of like an assault, you know": Media resisters' meta-decoding practices of media culture. *Critical Studies in Media Communication, 33*(5), 399–408. https://doi.org/10.1080/15295036.2016.1222076

Wukich, C. (2016). Social media use in emergency management. *Journal of Emergency Management, 13*(4), 281–294.

Xenos, M., Vromen, A., & Loader, B. D. (2014). The great equalizer? Patterns of social media use and youth political engagement in three advanced democracies, *Information, Communication & Society, 17*(2), 151–167. doi:10.1080/13691 18X.2013.871318

Yamamoto, M., Kushin, M.J., and Dalisay, F. (2013). Social media and mobiles as political mobilization forces for young adults: Examining the moderating role of online political expression in political participation. *New Media & Society*, (17), 880–898.

Younis, N. (2007). *War on Bloggers Unfolds.* Available at http://norayounis.net/2007/ 05/11/240

Yousef, S., & Nafisa, E. (2019). *Sudan restricts social media access to counter-protest movement.* Hopkins University Press.

Index

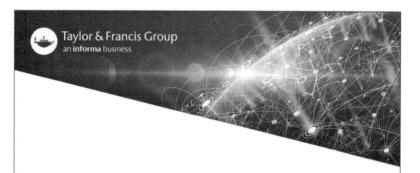